Abraham Ribicoff
and Jon O. Newman

POLITICS: The
American
Way

1967 ALLYN AND BACON, INC.

Boston   Rockleigh, N. J.   Atlanta   Dallas   Belmont, Calif.

ABOUT THE AUTHORS

Abraham Ribicoff is United States Senator from Connecticut. A graduate of the University of Chicago Law School, he has served in as great a variety of public offices as any man in American political life. In his home state he has been a member of the legislature, a municipal court judge, and was twice elected Governor. On the national scene he has been a Congressman, Secretary of the Department of Health, Education, and Welfare, and since 1963 a member of the U. S. Senate. In addition to eight political campaigns of his own, he has participated in numerous campaigns for other local, state, and national candidates, including a key role in the nomination and election of President John F. Kennedy.

Jon O. Newman is United States Attorney for the District of Connecticut. A graduate of Princeton University and Yale Law School, he has served with Mr. Ribicoff in the Governor's office in Connecticut, the Department of Health, Education, and Welfare, and the U. S. Senate. He directed Mr. Ribicoff's Senate campaign in 1962. Formerly a senior law clerk to Chief Justice Earl Warren, he has also been a member of the graduate faculty of Trinity College in Hartford, Connecticut.

Abraham Lincoln once observed that the United States has ". . . a system of political institutions, conducing more essentially to the ends of civil and religious liberty, than any of which the history of former times tells us." This was true in Lincoln's day, and it remains true today. Our political institutions and traditions possibly give us a truer democracy and a fuller freedom than has been given to any other people.

But we have no gratuitous guarantee that this great American heritage will continue forever. The United States is free and dynamic only because the American people have governed themselves with wisdom and foresight. Our foreign and domestic policies have been successful only because they have been formulated by enlightened men and women.

This means that America's future will be guaranteed only if the most able and dedicated of our young people enter politics. It also requires that those who do not enter public service at least concern themselves with public affairs. You, the reader of this book, represent America's future — our country will be what you help make it.

Abraham Ribicoff, a former state legislator, judge, Congressman, Governor, member of the President's Cabinet, and now United States Senator, is uniquely qualified to know politics in all its varied dimensions. His well-written book is an excellent introduction to the political life of our country. It helps us understand why people vote as they do, how candidates are nominated, how they campaign, and why some are elected while others fail. We are told about political parties and political partisans in an authoritative yet interesting manner. These are subjects which we must all understand a little better if we are to fulfill our obligation to America.

Hubert H. Humphrey

ABOUT THE BOOK

The American federal system of government is often the despair of many of our foreign friends who seek to comprehend it. At the national level they are confused by the complex system of checks and balances. And as they move on to study the state and county and city and lesser levels they are all but lost in the infinite variety and overlapping jurisdictions.

But there is indeed method in what some observers consider the American political madness. What the uninitiated observer may see as unnecessary complexities of the American system may well be the channels which provide for the widest possible citizen participation or the very fences of freedom itself.

In arguing the merits of his own system of government the American enjoys a singular advantage: unrivaled success. Though a relative newcomer to the political state the American has demonstrated through 19 decades a rare ability to adapt himself and his political institutions to a changing economic and international environment.

And, while doing so, his people have enjoyed a measure of justice, order, liberty and prosperity unmatched in the recorded history of man.

In this brief book, Senator Ribicoff has successfully charted the labyrinth through which American politicians must travel to local, state and national power. He is uniquely qualified to act as a guide in that labyrinth.

One of the most respected and able Senators on the Democratic side of the aisle, he previously has served as Governor of the State of Connecticut and as Secretary of Health, Education and Welfare in the Cabinet of the late President John F. Kennedy.

In these pages he has performed a public service. For it is through a greater understanding of the manner in which they are governed that young American men and women will inevitably be drawn to greater participation in the political management of their own affairs.

Richard Nixon

PREFACE

This is a book about politics, politicians, and political life. It seeks to combine the learning of political science with the reality of political experience. The range is broad—from the history of political parties to the structure of party organizations, from the mechanics of the voting process to an analysis of voter behavior, from the motivation of political candidates to the strategy and conduct of political campaigns. The focus is national, state, and local, and illustrative examples are chosen from all parts of the country.

The idea and need for this book were suggested to us by the publisher. We hope the material will be of interest to the working politician, the citizen who observes and participates in politics, and the student of government, civics, or American history.

We are most grateful to Vice President Hubert H. Humphrey and former Vice President Richard M. Nixon for their suggestions and introductory remarks. Valuable research assistance was rendered by Wayne Granquist, John O'Sullivan, and Judith Mazo of Senator Ribicoff's office and Walter Kravitz of the Library of Congress. We received skillful editorial suggestions from Natalie Spingarn of the Senator's staff. Helen Hill performed yeoman service preparing the manuscript. Our wives, with patience, indulgence, and understanding, permitted us the years of experience and the months of writing that comprise this book, and we are appreciative beyond words.

Views and opinions of thousands of professional and amateur politicians are reflected in these pages, but the responsibility for all of the thoughts expressed is entirely our own.

A.R.

J.O.N.

Hartford, Connecticut.
1966.

CONTENTS

1

WHAT
IS
POLITICS?

A high school student somewhere in this country right now is one day going to be President of the United States. That is at once the most inevitable and the most promising fact of American politics.

Many others will be Governors, Senators, Congressmen, members of state legislatures, mayors, and city councilmen. Still others will be national, state, or local chairmen of the Republican and Democratic parties — or perhaps of new third parties, delegates to national conventions, or members of local party committees. Some will manage election campaigns, raise funds, write speeches, canvass voters, recruit volunteer campaign workers, or work at polling places on election day. Most will become members of a political party. Almost all will be voters. Together they will produce the politics of their generation.

As the students of today become the adult citizens of tomorrow, they will be involved with politics in many activities. In business it will be necessary to choose a company president. A labor union must select officers. Leaders must be chosen for each local charitable and religious organization, each civic and fraternal club, even country clubs and community centers. Students first acquire experience in selecting leaders when they choose their class president and other class officers, their club leaders, or the captain of the football team.

Sometimes the election process simply calls for a show of hands. More often the size of the group requires some more formal procedure. So rules are developed to provide for nominations and elections. Once this much of a framework is established, an informal process begins to develop that indicates whether candidates will seek support, how and when they will campaign, and how their supporters and opponents will organize. The greater the power to be handed to the winner, the more elaborate will be the method to determine his selection. Whether the process is simple or elaborate, it will be political—that is, it will concern itself with relationships among people as they go about the important task of selecting those who will exercise governing power.

Once people have decided to organize local, state, and national governments, it becomes necessary to decide who will be given the right to exercise governmental or public power. A system of politics then develops in which these decisions affecting public power are made. It is this area of public politics—the system in which people select public officials—that we will be concerned with in this book.

The process of politics must answer certain specific questions. There are elections to decide who will hold public office. Who can vote? How are votes to be cast? What methods will be used to persuade voters to support the various candidates? How will candidates be nominated to compete in the election? The political process also needs political parties—a mechanism for continuing between elections the opposition between supporters of one candidate and supporters of other candidates. But who are party members? How do the parties govern themselves? How do they function?

Politics also has broader concerns, especially in a governmental system founded on principles of democracy. The political system must educate. It must help to make the people aware of their government and of the issues public officials will decide. It must also help to frame these issues for rational decision by the public so that the views of the people can have an appropriate bearing on the decision-making of their government. If politics is to serve the people well, it must be a constantly improving process, raising the sights and standards of its participants to better the process of government itself.

Politics deals basically with people. All of politics involves relationships among people, supporting each other in common cause, or opposing each other in electoral battle. There are really two sets of political relationships—between politicians and the public, and between the politicians themselves. Men and women in politics, whether in elective office or not, are constantly concerned with what the public is thinking, what the public wants, what the public is likely to accept or reject in the future. The politician who fails to pay close attention to the public finds himself out of politics very soon. To know the public, the politician must seek out the people, meet them everywhere, listen to them, argue with them, learn from them, and react to them. Sometimes he must follow them. Often he must lead them.

For their part, the people must maintain a relationship with the politicians. They do this periodically by voting, but more is required. People must keep tabs on their public officials, pay attention to the voting records of their Senators, Congressmen, state legislators, and city councilmen. They should not hesitate to express their approval or disapproval about what the politicians do. After all, it is their business—the public business—that is being transacted. To keep the political system ever responsive to popular will, people have to participate in the system. This means joining a political party, attending local political meetings, volunteering time during campaigns, voting in party primary elections, and in every way exercising a citizen's full say in the conduct of affairs within the political party of his choice.

The relationships between politicians themselves rest upon trust, loyalty, and understanding. In the world of politics there are no written contracts, no courts to enforce business agreements. A politician's only bond is his word. Of course, not all politicians have a reputation for trustworthiness, just as there are unreliable people in every line of endeavor. But probably no form of human activity exceeds politics in the number of significant decisions that are sealed only with a man's word and his handshake. Whether it is a party leader promising support to a candidate or a Senator promising the President to vote for a bill, the politician's word is all that is given, but it is relied upon. A politician who breaks his word rarely survives in politics long enough to see if anyone will trust him again.

Loyalty among politicians runs deep. The support of a delegate in a convention fight for a nomination will be remembered by the winning candidate for the rest of his political life. When that delegate needs help in his own political struggles, he can count on the man whose loyalty he has earned.

The relationships between politicians extend across party lines. Many politicians count among their closest friends leading figures in opposing political parties. Often spectators in the galleries of the U. S. Congress are surprised to see two opposing legislators vigorously assail each other in debate and then walk to the cloakroom together, chatting amiably one friend to another. They take their political differences seriously. But they recognize that however strongly each feels about his position, the other has some reasonable basis for the position he is urging, and both, as elected officials, have different constituencies to represent. Almost every politician, whether officeholder or not, recognizes in other politicians men and women who have become actively involved in a difficult undertaking, and they respect each other for the strength of their convictions.

Of course, the political world is not all sweetness and light. People are competing for high stakes, and the goal of winning, whether a precinct leadership or the Presidency, sometimes brings out selfish instincts. Politics, like life itself, has its cruel side. There are personal attacks and bitter disappointments. It is not a field for the thin-skinned. There are times when the public interest is crassly disregarded by men of greed and selfishness. Shabby deals are made in backrooms. Some campaign speeches rival in preposterousness the promises of a sideshow barker.

But there is a noble side as well. The world of politics includes courage, idealism, and selfless dedication to the well-being of all mankind. And if there are a few villains in the plot, they count for little when the heroes are an Adlai E. Stevenson, a Robert A. Taft, and a John F. Kennedy. Politics offers excitement, stimulation, and challenge. There is an abundance of opportunity waiting to be realized by each generation. If you have energy, talent, and ambition, there is no limit to the heights you can reach or the useful tasks you can accomplish.

The political system that each generation inherits will be intrinsically neither good nor bad. Its quality will depend on the people who participate in it, and on the demands and expectations of the public at large.

For various reasons the word "politics" often has an unfavorable connotation. Very likely this stems from the history of graft and corruption associated with the politics of our country's earlier days. Isolated instances of such activity still occur, but not often. The ethics of today's politicians compare favorably with the ethics of those engaged in other endeavors.

Then, too, the label "political" is used critically to characterize any action by a politician that is designed to win him popular support. A legislator's vote on a bill will be derisively called "political" by those who mean that he abandoned personal convictions and voted instead to do what was popular with the voters. Sometimes a legislator should be criticized for giving in to popular pressures. Yet the fact that he did what his constituents wanted is surely not always to be condemned, especially in a democracy.

Finally, the adverse connotation of "political" stems in part from its traditional application to those who are engaged in the conduct of party matters, as distinguished from officeholders. The precinct captain or the national chairman is known as a politician; the state legislator or the U. S. Senator prefers to be considered a "statesman." The truth is that every person who participates in the political system, whether as a party worker or an elected official, is a politician and should be proud of it. He may do some things properly criticized as "too political." He may also be hailed for doing something statesmanlike. But all politicians, the good ones, the bad ones, the dedicated and the greedy, the idealists and the pragmatists—all make the political system work. And what they do determines what kind of a system we will have, what kind of government we will select, and in what kind of country we will live. Can there be a more important task?

Like all other Americans, the generation now coming of age will take the political system and adapt it to its own purposes. There will be no revolutionary change. Our political system has too much history, too much tradition, too many people actively involved, and too much scattering of power to permit any drastic changes to occur in a hurry. But little changes happen all the time. Every person has the power to make his personal impact on the system. The force and direction of all the personal impacts of all our citizens will determine the kind of political system this generation of Americans will pass on to the next.

2

THE

VOTERS

In the privacy of the polling booth the voters become the most important people in politics. They give power, they take away power, they elect, they re-elect, and they defeat. And no matter what answer they give, their vote gives them the right to give another answer every one, two, four, or, at most, six years. The voters have the real power — and the politicians know it.

Who can vote? Who does vote? Why do we vote as we do? These are questions that concern every candidate, every office-holder, and every political leader. Only recently have we learned very much about the behavior of the American voter, and even what is known has been slow in coming to the attention of most politicians.

WHO CAN VOTE?

Americans are proud of their democratic form of government, and surely the essence of democracy is the direct say that the people have in running their government — national, state, and local. Today, we take for granted the idea that in a democracy everybody can vote. It is true that almost every adult in this country can vote, but we have been a long time making this idea a reality.

The power to decide who can vote rests with each of the 50 states, but this power must be exercised within the limits of both the United States Constitution and the laws Congress has passed to make sure the Constitutional rules are obeyed. For example, the 15th Amendment directs that the right to vote shall not be denied "on account of race, color, or previous condition of servitude," and the 19th Amendment forbids voting discrimination based on

Crowds waiting to vote in the South, now include substantial numbers of Negro voters, a result due in part to Federal election laws passed between 1957 and 1965.

sex. As long as the Constitutional rules are followed, however, each state is free to set its own qualifications for voters. Eligibility to vote has been broadened almost continuously throughout our country's history.

Property Qualifications. In our country's earliest days, the right to vote was sharply limited. In some states the voters amounted to less than 3 percent of the population. Most of the original 13 states required a person to own a certain amount of property or to pay a certain amount of taxes before he was eligible to vote. By 1850, almost all of the states abandoned these qualifications and extended suffrage—the right to vote—to all adult free males.

Negroes. The next major extension of the right to vote began in 1863 when the Emancipation Proclamation freed the Negro slaves. By the end of the Civil War, some Northern states had voluntarily granted Negroes the right to vote, but the Federal Constitution did not guarantee this right in all the states until the 15th Amendment was adopted in 1870.

While the 15th Amendment proclaimed a national policy against restricting the Negroes' right to vote, Negro suffrage did not become a reality in all parts of the country. The Reconstruction period saw a temporary surge of Negro voting in the South backed by Federal troops and Northern carpetbaggers. In five Southern states, Negro voters actually outnumbered white voters. Negroes were elected to state legislatures, to the U. S. House of Representatives, and to the U. S. Senate.

The withdrawal of Federal troops in 1877 marked the end of Reconstruction and the beginning of a sharp decline in Negro voting. Through such tactics as gerrymandering,[1] poll taxes, literacy tests, and outright intimidation, Southern whites succeeded in nullifying the Negroes' right to vote. Even where Negroes managed to register for elections, the Democratic Party in some Southern states effectively barred them from any meaningful say in politics by limiting the all-important primaries to white voters. These primaries are election contests at which the party membership chooses party candidates for the general election.

As World War II ended, the Negroes' right to vote began moving from theory to practice. In 1944, the U. S. Supreme Court ruled that white primaries were in violation of the 15th Amendment.[2] In 1957, Congress passed the first Civil Rights Act since Reconstruction. Part of this law permits the U. S. Attorney General to get a court order to stop anyone who interferes with another person's right to vote. This Act was followed, in 1960, by additional legislation which provided that Federal voting referees could be appointed

---

[1] The term "gerrymandering" originated in Massachusetts in 1812, where the supporters of Governor Elbridge Gerry redrew the lines of the state's legislative districts to strengthen his party's control of the legislature. One district was so irregularly drawn it resembled a salamander. "No," said a newspaper editor, "it is a Gerrymander."

This practice has been extended, and the lines of election districts have been redrawn in such a way as to give an advantage to some groups of voters at the expense of others. To reduce the voting strength of Negroes, for example, a district line would be drawn down the middle of an area where many Negro voters lived. Their voting strength would thus be divided into two districts where they would be a minority in each, whereas they would have constituted a majority if they all had been included in either of the two districts. In 1963, the U. S. Supreme Court ruled that drawing election-district lines on the basis of the voters' race was unconstitutional. But state legislatures frequently draw election-district lines in irregular fashion in hopes of gaining advantage for one of the political parties.

[2] *Smith* v. *Allright*, 321 U. S. 649 (1944).

by the Federal Courts to register voters in those districts where a pattern of discrimination could be proved. One portion of the comprehensive Civil Rights Act of 1964 further protected the right to vote by preventing the discriminatory use of literacy tests. It provided that everyone who has completed the sixth grade shall, generally, be considered to be capable of reading and writing without the need for a test of reading ability. Also in 1964, the 24th Amendment to the Constitution was adopted, prohibiting the payment of a poll tax as a requirement for voting in all elections for Federal offices.

In 1965, Congress took the strongest action it had ever taken to make sure Negroes could vote. The Voting Rights Act passed that year cut through the legal technicalities of earlier laws and simply abolished literacy tests in election districts (mostly in the South) where registration was so low that past discrimination against Negroes was obvious. In addition, the U. S. Attorney General was given the power to send Federal voting registrars to these districts. The results were dramatic. In some counties where only a handful of Negroes had ever previously been allowed to register with state officials, the Federal registrars quickly enrolled thousands of Negro voters. In 1966, the U. S. Supreme Court took another helpful step by ruling that payment of poll taxes as a condition for voting was unconstitutional in any kind of election.

The result of all these efforts has been an increase in the number of Negro voters in the South from about 250,000 in 1940 to 2,500,000 in 1966.

Women. Women spurred their efforts to win the right to vote in the post-Civil War period. But, by World War I, only a handful of states had yielded to feminine persuasion. A militant campaign began during 1917, including protest marches, picketing of the White House, and hunger strikes by jailed suffragettes. Woodrow Wilson finally gave the ladies his support in 1919, and the following year the 19th Amendment was adopted, assuring citizens the right to vote regardless of sex.

The District of Columbia. In the nation's capital, the voters are not permitted to elect local officeholders. Home-rule proposals to correct this situation are regularly presented to Congress but, thus far, without success. Also, since the District is not a state, the

Although some states gave women the right to vote before the turn of the century, women's suffrage throughout the nation did not become a reality until 1920.

residents do not elect any Representatives or Senators to Congress.

Prior to 1964, District of Columbia residents were so disenfranchised that they could not even vote in presidential elections. The District had no votes in the electoral college, the assembly of men and women elected by the voters of each state, who officially elect the President and Vice President of the United States. The 23rd Amendment, adopted in 1964, corrected this inadequacy. It gives the District of Columbia the same number of presidential electors as the smallest state (normally three), thus giving the residents of the District the opportunity to vote in presidential elections.

State Restrictions. These historic developments have moved the nation toward the democratic ideal of universal suffrage. There are, however, several restrictions imposed by the states under their powers to set voter qualifications. These state restrictions, of course, cannot undermine the extensions of the right to vote that have been written into the Constitution and the laws of the United States.

Age. The most obvious restriction concerns voting age. Almost all the states accept 21 as the minimum voting age, though Hawaii uses 20, Alaska 19, and Georgia and Kentucky 18.

Efforts to lower the voting age to 18 have won the support of such national leaders as Presidents Eisenhower and Kennedy. A compelling argument is made that those who are old enough to fight and die for their country are old enough to vote for their country's leaders. But most states have been persuaded to keep the voting age at the level of legal adulthood.

Citizenship. All the states limit the right to vote to citizens of the United States. Curiously, this is one area of election law where the trend has been to narrow eligibility requirements. Earlier in our history many states allowed aliens to vote, especially those who had taken a first step toward becoming citizens. It was not until 1928 that a national election was held in which no state permitted aliens to vote.

Residence. Residence requirements are in force in all states, with most requiring residence of one year before a person can vote in a state election, and usually a much shorter period of residency to vote in a local election. Because so many Americans move, these residence laws make many people ineligible to vote. In 1964, an estimated 5 million people were unable to vote for President because of failure to meet residence requirements. The trend is to reduce the residence time for voting in a presidential election, and some states do permit new residents to vote in presidential elections. Wisconsin, for example, lets newcomers vote if they were qualified to vote in the state from which they moved. Connecticut lets those who move out of the state vote by absentee ballot for two years, unless they register in the new state.

Residence requirements are designed to insure that people who move into a new state, or a new community within a state, live there long enough to learn about local matters before they vote for local officeholders. A period of three months, seems adequate for this purpose in state and local elections. In national elections the reason for a residence requirement seems to be insubstantial. Is a voter less competent to decide knowledgeably about his choice for President just because he has moved from one state to another?

Literacy. Literacy tests are in use in about one-third of the states. They generally require only the ability to read, but sometimes they include a test of a person's ability to explain the meaning of some part of the state constitution. For years these tests were used in a discriminatory way to keep Negroes in the South from registering and, thus, prevent them from voting. The Civil Rights Act of 1964 and the Voting Rights Act of 1965 helped to correct this abuse. In election districts where less than 50% of the voting-age population was registered in November 1964 or voted in the presidential election that year, literacy tests have been abolished.

Other Restrictions. Most of the states disqualify people from voting for reasons such as insanity, conviction of a felony, or imprisonment. Among the odd restrictions is a Florida law, not vigorously enforced, that keeps a person from voting if he has made a bet on the election!

Registration. A final restriction on voting is the registration process. In most states, every voter must be registered. This simply means that sometime before election day he must satisfy the local election officials that he meets all the eligibility requirements. His name then appears on the list of eligible voters, entitling him to cast a ballot on election day.

Most states have permanent registration: once a voter is registered, he need not register again as long as he lives in the same election district. But in a few states a person must register over again at regular intervals, such as every four years. Some states take a voter's name off the registration list if he has failed to vote in recent elections.

In some communities registration is permitted on only a limited number of days and, then, only at a limited number of locations, perhaps only at the city hall. Seventeen states permit registration by mail. The inconvenience of registering discourages a sizeable number of people from bothering to qualify for the right to vote.

WHO DOES VOTE?

Most Americans can vote, but the plain truth is that most of them don't, at least not regularly. In presidential elections, voter-turnout among all adults who could have qualified to vote has ranged from a high of 85% in 1876 to a low of 44% in 1920. The percentage gradually increased to just over 60% in 1952 where it has remained. These are national percentages. There is extraordinary variation among the states. In 1960, voter-turnout ranged from 25% in Mississippi to 80% in Idaho.

In non-presidential election years, the national voter-turnout rate has never reached 50%. In local elections and in primaries the rate drops far lower. Compared with many other countries our voter-turnout record is not good. In many European countries voter-turnout usually exceeds 70% and has topped 90% in Italy. Some countries make voting much easier than it is in the United States. Some hold elections on Sunday, a day when most people are not working; others make registration procedures so simple that virtually all adults register. Australia, New Zealand, and a few European countries make voting compulsory by law. The penalty for not voting is usually a modest fine, which is rarely imposed, or public posting of the names of the nonvoters. Compulsory voting requirements, however, do not seem to have much effect on voter-turnout. Indeed, we may ask whether voting should be a duty imposed by law, or a privilege available to those who wish to use it.

Why are there so many nonvoters in the United States? What prevents or discourages people from voting? Some run into legal disqualifications, especially residence requirements. Some are away from their communities on election day and either forget or are unable to secure an absentee ballot. Many forget or are too lazy to register. Some find the location of polling places or the hours they are open too inconvenient. In states and communities where one party traditionally wins a much heavier vote than the other, many voters in the dominant party feel their votes are not needed, and those in the minority party feel their votes are useless.

Studies of voters tell a good deal about the characteristics of those who vote. Voter-turnout among men is generally 10% higher than among women. Those above age 35 vote with more regularity than those younger than 35. The voter-turnout rate among high-income families is much higher than among low-income families, and also higher among those with a college education compared to those who attended only grade school.[3]

Voter-turnout. Voter-turnout has tremendous significance

---

[3] Angus Campbell, P. Converse, W. Miller, and D. Stokes, *The American Voter* (New York: John Wiley & Sons, Inc., 1960), pp. 478, 484, 495. Austin Ranney, *The Governing of Men* (New York: Holt, Rinehart & Winston, Inc., 1958), pp. 291–93.

APATHY

Public Enemy No. 1

James J. Dobbins, *The Boston Herald Traveler*

for the outcome of elections. By election day practically everyone's mind is made up. The only remaining question is how many will actually get to the polls to record their votes. In many elections, the number of eligible voters who fail to vote far exceeds the number of voters who switch their support from one side to the other during the campaign. In other words, if one party could bring to the polls every eligible person who would vote for its candidates, it could win many elections without bothering to campaign at all. Of course this never happens. What often decides elections is which party can get out the largest share of its potential strength.

Every Vote Counts. Bringing that last voter to the polls is often crucial, for many elections are amazingly close. If James G. Blaine had received one more vote in every precinct of New York, in 1884, he would have been elected President over Grover Cleveland. One added vote per precinct in California, in 1916, would have enabled Charles Evans Hughes to defeat Woodrow Wilson.

The distribution of the votes is all important in a presidential election, where the candidate with the most votes in a state wins all the electoral votes of that state. A switch of one vote in half the precincts in Ohio and California, in 1948, would have kept Harry Truman from receiving a majority of the electoral votes and thrown the election into the House of Representatives. In 1960, when more than 68 million people voted in the presidential contest, only 118,550 more votes were cast for Kennedy than for Nixon. If Nixon had won the states of Illinois and Texas with their 51 electoral votes—he lost Illinois by 8,500 votes and Texas by 46,000 votes—he would have won a majority of the nation's electoral votes by 270–252, instead of losing by 303–219.

Even narrower margins have decided some state elections. The Governor of Michigan was elected, in 1950, by a margin of one vote in every three precincts in the state. The margin of victory for the Kansas Governor, in 1940, was one vote in every six precincts. In 1962, the Governor of Minnesota won election by the slim margin of 91 votes out of 1,240,000. Senators and Congressmen have also won eyelash victories, but the all-time classic case is the Connecticut state representative who won his primary by one vote, and then won the general election—also by just one vote!

> *On election day in November, 1876, a sick man in Indiana insisted that he be brought to the polls to cast his vote. The Congressman he supported won that election by one vote. That Congressman soon found himself appointed to a 15-man commission assembled to settle electoral vote disputes in the presidential contest between Samuel J. Tilden and Rutherford B. Hayes. The Congressman voted to award the disputed votes to Hayes. The Commission agreed with him, by a margin of 8 to 7. Their decision confirmed the election of President Hayes by an electoral vote margin of 185 to 184.*

WHY PEOPLE VOTE

Only in recent years has any systematic effort been made to find out why people vote as they do. One way to find out is to ask, yet this is exactly what most politicians fail to do. In the heat of an election campaign, they are too busy; when it is over, they are either too delighted, or disappointed, to spend the time and money to find out something more than the bare result of who won. This task of investigating voter-behavior has been taken up by a few college professors and pollsters. The result has been the gathering, especially since 1940, of much useful information about voters and their voting patterns.[4]

Opinion Polls. Our chief source of information about voters and their voting patterns has been the public opinion poll. While politicians enjoy scoffing at polls (especially those that show their side is losing), the fact is that polls have become increasingly reliable and relied upon.

Many people in and out of politics are quick to dismiss the accuracy of polls by pointing to the 1948 election when President Truman upset the predictions of almost every pollster by defeating Thomas E. Dewey. But the pollsters of 1948 erred not in their polling techniques but in their failure to continue polling right up until the election. Their early predictions of a Dewey victory were probably correct as of the day their polls were taken. Failure to poll during the last six weeks of the campaign missed the decisive shift of popular sentiment to Truman. With this glaring exception, scientific political polls in this country and abroad have consistently shown a high degree of accuracy, especially in national elections. Rarely have national election results varied from pollsters' predictions by more than 3%.

The accuracy of polls rests on the principle of sampling. A winetaster needs only a sip from a barrel of wine to make a judgment about the quality of the contents of the entire barrel. Sampling wine is almost 100% reliable because each sip from the barrel is just like every other sip. Suppose, however, we have a bag of 100 marbles, some red and some blue. Can we predict with any accuracy how

---

[4] See Paul F. Lazarsfield, B. Berelson, and H. Gaudet, *The People's Choice* (New York: Duell, Sloan & Pearce, 1944); B. Berelson, P. Lazarsfield, and W. McPhee, *Voting* (Chicago: University of Chicago Press, 1954); Angus Campbell, Gerald Gurin, and Warren Miller, *The Voter Decides* (Evanston, Ill.: Row, Peterson and Company, 1954); Angus Campbell, P. Converse, W. Miller, and D. Stokes, *The American Voter* (New York: John Wiley & Sons, Inc., 1960); David Wallace, *First Tuesday* (Garden City, N.Y.: Doubleday & Company, Inc., 1964).

many of the marbles are red? If we reach in and take out a handful of 20, this sample may show 15 red and 5 blue marbles. Since 75% of our sample are red marbles, can we predict that 75% of all the marbles in the bag are red? If our sample handful had come out 16 red and 4 blue, could we have predicted that 80% of the total would be red? An actual count of all the marbles shows 75 red and 25 blue. Our 80%-red prediction would have been in error by 5%, but we would still have learned, just from our sample, without looking at the rest, that a large majority of all the marbles in that bag were red.

One of the most famous failures in predicting election results tells us a great deal about the method and high reliability of modern public opinion polling.

In 1936, a popular magazine, The Literary Digest, *conducted a "poll" to predict the outcome of the presidential contest between Franklin D. Roosevelt and Alfred M. Landon, The* Digest *made no effort to seek the opinions of a representative sample of American voters. Instead, the magazine mailed more than 10 million ballots to names compiled from telephone directories and automobile registration files. More than 2 million people filled out these ballots and mailed them back to the magazine.*

The Digest *"poll" was doomed to failure because it sought the opinion only of those groups who supported Landon. In 1936, owners of telephones and cars were found primarily in the ranks of middle- and upper-income families and less frequently among the poor. As the Gallup Poll pointed out at the time, Landon was drawing support from 59% of telephone owners but only 18% of people on relief.*

Based on 2 million ballots from an unrepresentative sample, The Literary Digest *predicted Roosevelt would lose with only 40.9% of the popular vote. Instead, he won in a landslide with 60.2%*

The Gallup Poll, using a small but scientifically selected sample, not only correctly predicted Roosevelt's victory, but also predicted within 1% the margin of error of the Digest "poll," even before the magazine had mailed out its ballots!

Obviously, sampling is accurate only if the sample has the same characteristics in the same proportion as are found in the "universe" from which the sample is drawn. In the marble case, we had only two characteristics, redness and blueness. When we sample voters and try to make predictions about the results of a forthcoming election, the problem becomes much more complicated because there are so many different characteristics of people. And in sampling voters, we add an important assumption: that a voter with one set of characteristics — age, sex, religion, race, income, education, geography, occupation, etc. — will vote the same way as most other voters with the same characteristics. The problem is to select a sample of voters whose characteristics fairly reflect the entire voting population. For example, if 10% of all voters are Negroes, an accurate sample of 1,000 voters must include 100 Negroes among other characteristics similar to the entire voting population. Most voter samples range from 300 to 2,000 voters. If the sample is carefully selected, the pollsters can be quite sure that the sample will reflect the views of the city, state, or nation from which the sample was drawn.

The polls that tell something about voter-behavior are in some respects more informative than the more publicized polls that predict election results.

Polls that try to predict election results encounter two problems. First, they depend on a man's own statement of what he is going to do in the future. He may not know, or he may in fact do something different from what he honestly thought he was going to do. Second, while most polls have in recent years achieved a high degree of accuracy — often within 2 or 3 percentage points of the outcome — they still miss some forecasts for the simple reason that many elections are decided by a margin of not more than 2 or 3 percentage points. In 1948 the Gallup Poll prediction of the winner in that presidential election was off by only 5% but Truman's margin over Dewey was just 4%.

On the other hand, polls that investigate general voting patterns instead of predicting specific election results escape these two dangers. These voter-behavior polls secure much of their information by asking people for facts: "Whom did you vote for in the last four elections?" rather than "Whom are you going to vote for this year?" An error of 2 or 3 percentage points hardly matters in most inquiries of voter-behavior. When we learn, for example, that about

75% of the people support the same party that their parents supported, the fact is of interest and importance even though the exact percentage may really be 73 or 77. **What the Polls Show.** The public opinion studies have rudely shocked us out of the civics-book dreamworld where every voter awaits each election with interest, sizes up each candidate, learns about the issues, follows the campaign, and then makes up his mind.

In the real world of voters, some know nothing about elections, most have their minds made up on a partisan basis before the candidates are even chosen, and of those who do decide during a campaign, some are the least interested in the outcome.

There are, of course, some voters in every election who do select the candidate of their choice solely on the issues and the campaign, but they are usually a small minority.

And there are some elections in which the campaign, or the events of the day, or the personal appeal of the candidate makes a strong impact and causes a substantial number of voters to make their decision irrespective of party lines. President Eisenhower, in 1952, clearly won the votes of many Democrats who felt a successful war hero could end the Korean conflict. President Johnson, in 1964, was supported by many Republicans who were opposed to the conservative views of Barry Goldwater. But these are the exceptions that prove the rule of most elections: campaigns switch a small percentage of the voters.

Even the unprecedented margin achieved by Lyndon Johnson in 1964 was not, according to the polls, the result of anything that happened during the campaign period. The polls showed no significant change from the start of the campaign right up to the election and were very accurate in predicting the outcome. (See the chart on page 20.)

Whatever factors produced the landslide of 1964 — the records and stands of the candidates, the events of the day, the circumstances under which Johnson became President — it is apparent that the events of the campaign period were not what caused so many voters to depart from their normal voting patterns.

Public Awareness. Public awareness of candidates, campaigns, and issues, while increasing all the time, is often surprisingly lacking. In one study, 65% of the voters who were asked to name their two U. S. Senators were unable to do so.[5]

	Johnson	Goldwater	Undecided
Harris Poll taken after Republican Convention, July 1964	62%	31%	7%
Harris Poll, election eve	62%	33%	5%
Harris Poll and Gallup Poll, election eve, with undecided vote allocated between the candidates	64%	36%	
Actual results (National popular vote)	61.4%	38.6%	

Another index of low voter-awareness is the support given to unknown candidates who have the same name as a popular figure. In 1958, a political unknown won nomination and election to the office of state treasurer in Massachusetts, with one major asset: his name happened to be John F. Kennedy.

Party Support.   A more significant fact is the large proportion of voters who support their political party no matter who the candidates are. On the basis of party affiliation, nearly one-half, and in some elections about three-fourths, of the voters are prepared to announce their voting choice before candidates are even nominated.[6] And in most elections, an even higher percentage end up voting for the candidate of the party that normally commands their allegiance.

Of course, party preferences do change over a period of years. In the late 1920's and early 1930's, many city voters became Demo-

---

[5] Hadley Cantril, ed., *Public Opinion* (Princeton, N.J.: Princeton University Press, 1951), p. 790.

[6] Wallace, *First Tuesday*, pp. 137 – 38.

crats, in part because they believed the Democratic Party would help end widespread unemployment. In the late 1950's and early 1960's, many Southern voters switched their allegiance to the Republican Party. In the cities and suburbs, they switched because they favored more progressive policies than those of the Democratic city organizations; in the rural areas, many became Republicans to protest efforts of the Democratic Party nationally to end racial segregation.

In addition to these gradual shifts, some voters desert their parties in particular elections and for particular candidates, as we have seen in the national elections of 1952 and 1964. But despite exceptions, the pattern of regular party voting is one of the central facts of American politics.

To learn more about this pattern of party voting we must understand the grouping of voters within the major parties. Several studies have divided voters into groups according to age, sex, education, religion, occupation, income, and residence. Clear patterns emerge. For example, most people in professional jobs support Republican candidates and most unskilled workers support Democratic candidates. Most people from small towns vote Republican; most people from big cities vote Democratic.

When individual voters are grouped according to several common characteristics, the partisan voting pattern is even more constant. For example, if we examine the voting pattern of 100 voters, all of whom are doctors or lawyers, are Protestants, earn more than $20,000 a year, and live in midwestern cities smaller than 100,000 population, we will find that nearly all of them vote Republican. And they do so in every election, regardless of who the candidates are. On the other hand, if we look at another group of 100 voters, all of whom work in unskilled jobs, are Catholic, earn less than $4,000 a year, and live in northeastern cities larger than 1 million population, we will find that nearly all of this group vote Democratic. The first group will very likely vote Republican more regularly than a group of 100 voters whose only common characteristic is that each of them calls himself a Republican. And the second group will just as likely vote Democratic more consistently than a miscellaneous assortment of 100 registered Democrats.

Why people with common characteristics vote alike is not fully understood. We do know that about 3 out of 4 voters support the same party that their parents supported.[7] This strongly suggests that party preference is influenced by the preference of one's parents. Another important influence on voter-behavior is the attitude of the dominant group in the community, which seems to remain strong from one election to the next. One study examined the popular vote in more than 2,000 counties over 9 presidential elections. In 70% of the more than 18,000 election results analyzed, each county supported the candidate of the same party it had supported in the previous election.[8] Apparently most of the people who grew up in those counties usually decided to vote the same way the majority had previously voted.

Very likely, the most important explanation for these group voting patterns is the fact that people with common characteristics have similar interests and similar attitudes about public issues. Voters who run businesses are interested in government policies that encourage more profits. Voters who are unemployed are interested in government policies that provide jobs. As the parties take positions on public issues, they tend to attract and hold the allegiance of those groups whose interests they support. If just one characteristic is analyzed, the group may be divided in party preference. For example, if we look at farmers as a voting group, we find that some support the Republican Party, while many others favor the Democrats. But the pattern becomes clearer when several characteristics are considered. Most farmers who are wealthy, midwestern, and over 60 years old vote Republican, while most farmers who are poor, Southern, and under 60 vote Democratic.

Bloc Voting.   These patterns of group voting are sometimes confused with what many politicians call bloc voting. By this they mean that members of a single group — usually a religious, racial, or ethnic group — can be expected to vote as a bloc. For example, most Negroes vote Democratic. However, they do so not because they are Negro, but because they favor government policies to promote equality of opportunity and to aid the poor, and they

---

[7] Campbell, *et al., The American Voter*, p. 147.

[8] Ralph and Mildred Fletcher, "Consistency in Party Voting, 1896–1932," *Social Forces*, XV (1936), pp. 281–85.

believe the Democratic Party supports such policies. Of course there are also many Negroes who believe the Republican Party supports such policies, and for this reason they vote Republican. On occasion bloc voting does occur when one candidate is of the same race, religion, or ethnic origin as a sizable group of voters. A Negro candidate was nearly elected mayor of Cleveland in 1965 because he won the votes of most of that city's Negroes. Some Catholic voters supported John F. Kennedy in 1960 primarily because he was a Catholic, while some Protestant voters opposed him primarily for this same reason. But this type of bloc voting, where a man's race, religion, or ethnic origin determines his vote, is of decreasing importance in modern America. More education and better communication have meant that an increased number of voters know more about their candidates than ever before. As a result, their vote is influenced more than ever before by the public positions and actions taken by the candidates and the parties. What remains true, however, is that groups of voters with the same economic and social characteristics usually agree on which party best serves the interests they favor. The result is a high degree of regular party voting.

The "Independent" Voter. What of the voters without a party allegiance? Who is that revered American phenomenon, the Independent Voter, free of party prejudice, proud of his record of voting for the "best man?"

Before this can be answered, there must be some agreement on terminology. At least two meanings of "independent" are involved. Some voters at the time of registration decline to list themselves officially as members of either major party. In Connecticut, for example, the unaffiliated group is larger than the membership of either party—about 40% of the total electorate. And in many states, registration laws make no provision for formal party enrollment. These independents are more accurately described as *unaffiliated* voters. Then, there are voters who like to think they choose the best man, regardless of his or their party. Such really *independent* voters are found among the registered members of both parties and also among the ranks of the unaffiliated.

The most significant fact about the unaffiliated voters is that their pattern of constant party voting is not too different from those

James J. Dobbins, *The Boston Herald Traveler*

who formally declare their party allegiance. One study has reported that two-thirds of the unaffiliated had always supported presidential candidates of the same political party. And about the same percentage were so committed to one of the two parties that they were sure how they would vote in a coming election before the candidates were even nominated.[9] Most of these voters are not "independent" in their voting pattern. They have a party allegiance; it is simply undeclared.

The really "independent" voter, who supports candidates regardless of party and regardless of his own declared or undeclared party affiliation, comes in two varieties. Many sincerely approach each election with an open mind and make their best judgment among the candidates. They read, listen, and think before they decide how to vote. But every voter study has shown that these real independents are a small part of the electorate.

Many others who claim to be "independent" in their voting are

---

[9] Wallace, *First Tuesday*, pp. 136–37.

voters who know least about the election, pay least attention to the campaign, and have least interest in the outcome. Many of them do not vote at all. Those who do often make up their minds late in the campaign and are easily swayed back and forth by the appeals of the candidates. These characteristics are found in many "independents," whether they are registered Republicans, registered Democrats, or unaffiliated.

How Many Switch? The number of voters who are open to persuasion in any campaign is much smaller than popularly assumed. Some studies have shown that less than 15% of the voters even considered voting for a candidate other than the one they were originally committed to by party preference. And the number that actually switch their preference from one candidate to the other during the typical campaign is even smaller.[10]

Even major electoral swings are surprisingly small in the percentage of switching voters. Two years after Eisenhower scored a landslide victory by winning 57% of the popular vote in 1956, the Democrats won a landslide in the Congressional elections of 1958, polling 56% of the vote. Yet, these two unusually large wins were the result of a net switch by only 13% of all the voters!

To see how this happened, let's look at the percent of the popular vote each party won in 1956 and 1958. The Republican percent dropped 13 points from 57 to 44, while the Democratic percent increased by the same amount, from 43 to 56. This meant that at least 13% of the voters left the Republican side and joined the Democratic side. There were probably a few Democratic voters in 1956 who switched against the trend in 1958 and voted Republican. Each of these switches cancelled out the effect of a 1956 Republican voter who shifted to the Democrats in 1958. So the 13% is the net switch of voters — all who shifted to the Democrats minus those few who shifted to the Republicans. The total percent who shifted in either direction from one election to the next is slightly higher, but most likely well under 20% of the total electorate.

Thus, a shift in voting strength from a landslide Republican win to a landslide Democratic win was accomplished by a switch in the individual voting patterns of a surprisingly small proportion of the

---

[10] Lazarsfield, *et al.*, *The People's Choice*, p.66.

nation's voters. If the Congressional vote totals of 1956 are compared with the 1958 totals, we find that the sizeable increase in seats won by the Democrats resulted from a net switch of only 5% of the voters.

Who Switches? The question then is: Who are the switchers? Here, we have to distinguish between those who switch party preference, and those who retain their party preference but split their ballot to support one or more candidates of the opposite party.

Sometimes, a group of voters, over a period time, will shift their party allegiance because of events of the day or actions of the party leaders in office. Many voters of German ancestry abandoned their support of the Democrats when the United States, provoked by submarine attacks, went to the aid of the Allies in World War I and declared war against Germany. Perhaps the most dramatic shift of a group of voters has involved the Negroes. Shortly after the Negroes were emancipated and won the right to vote, their political allegiance was strongly with the Republican Party of President Lincoln. This strong indentification lasted until the administration of Franklin D. Roosevelt. Then the policies of Democratic administrations gained the favor of Negro voters, until in the election of 1964, Negro voters were the strongest single group in their support of the Democratic presidential candidate. Many Negro districts gave President Johnson 95% of their votes.

Another cause of shifting party allegiance is less obvious. We have seen that party strength is based on the support of groups of voters with common characteristics. Sometimes, a voter with characteristics that normally show support of one party finds himself in a new situation where he acquires characteristics normally associated with support for the other party. Consider, for example, a poor girl from an Eastern city who marries a wealthy businessman and moves to a small Midwestern town. She is confronted with what political scientists call cross-pressures. She used to vote Democratic but she now leans towards the Republicans. Some of the voters in such situations will switch their party allegiance. Many will not finally decide which party they care to support, and will not vote at all. But it is changes of this sort—a new place to live, a new income level, a new job, or new relatives—that account for many changes in party preference.

Some who switch party preference do so because their allegiance is so weak that they are easily swayed back and forth between the parties. These voters are usually not well informed, take slight interest in politics, know little about candidates and issues, and are least exposed to political campaigning.[11] The problems they present for the campaigning candidates are obvious.

While the vast majority of voters retain their party preference from year to year, many voters are frequently willing to cross party lines to support at least one candidate of the opposite party. Their votes are often enough to supply the margin of victory. And because they are willing to split their ballot, they are open to the persuasion of each candidate's campaign. These ballot-splitters are the most crucial voters in American politics.

The Unpredictable Voter. These patterns of voting behavior apply to most people most of the time, especially in national elections. But in politics, as in life, nothing is certain. The history of politics is shot through with unexpected results. Sure winners have lost, unknowns have been elected, close contests have ended with landslides, and potentially big victories have been settled by a handful of votes. No politician will ever forget Harry Truman's upset victory over Thomas Dewey in 1948, nor will there ever be any doubt that it could happen again.

The weatherman may be able to predict when it will snow and how many inches will fall. But every single snowflake is unique, and no one can predict exactly what any one snowflake will look like or where it will fall.

Every politician also knows the individuality and unpredictability of the American voter. He knows that each voter is an individual human being and that no voter can ever be taken for granted. While election studies and polls can tell us something about the way people vote in the mass, they tell us little about a person's individual vote-decision, for that decision is a personal one.

It does happen that an individual voter will decide he likes a

[11] See Lazarsfield, *et al., The People's Choice,* p. 69; also Wallace, *First Tuesday,* p. 150.

Continual advances in the development of scientific polling techniques have greatly reduced the possibility of inaccuracies such as occurred in the 1948 presidential election.

particular candidate and vote for him regardless of party allegiance, regardless of past voting habits, regardless of anything predictable. Any one of several reasons may prompt this decision. The voter likes the candidate's looks; he hears a speech and is impressed; the candidate is a friend of his brother; his neighbor persuades him the day before election; he disapproves strongly of something the candidate's opponent has done; or he favors some course of action which the candidate has pledged to follow.

When we look at the whole field of politics, the important fact we discover is that usually a small percent of the voters makes such an unpredictable decision. Yet, when we look at any one election, the important fact is that a small number of votes generally decides who wins. So the few voters who switch, the few who are susceptible to the influence of a campaign can and, often, do decide who wins and who loses.

3

THE
CANDIDATES

The main event in politics is an election. Nothing else so dramatically focuses public attention upon the political process. Nothing else so forcefully gives the voters an immediate chance to participate in governmental affairs. No other event so clearly reduces to understandable terms the complex problems of a working democracy. To what extent the election successfully serves these purposes, indeed, to what extent democracy itself succeeds, depends in largest measure upon the men and women for whom the people vote—the candidates.

All candidates, not just those who win public office, shape our system of government. They present the voters with a choice, and upon their views and personalities depend the clarity and significance of that choice. They speak to the public during the weeks when attention is most easily focused upon public issues. They have the opportunity to educate, to lead in matters of public concern. Who they are, how they come to the fore, and why they run tell us much about the kind of political system we have.

CHARACTERISTICS OF CANDIDATES

The American people are a varied group, and their candidates for public office reflect this variety. Candidates come from all walks of life, with different backgrounds, experiences, qualifications, and personalities. There is no model candidate. Some, with all the apparent ingredients for success, have flopped; others, unheard of when they began, have won smashing victories. No matter what generalizations are made about candidates, the fact remains that any boy or girl in school right now might someday be a candidate.

Age, Sex, Religion, and National Origin. The Constitution sets minimum ages for Federal elective offices. The President must be 35, U. S. Senators must be 30, and members of the House of Representatives must be 25. Ted Kennedy became a Senator from Massachusetts when he was just 30. Francis Green retired as a Senator from Rhode Island at the age of 92. In 1965, the average age of U.S. Congressmen was 52, of U. S. Senators, 57, and of those elected to the House or the Senate for the first time, 43.

Before women acquired the right to vote in 1920, politics was a man's world. But soon after the ladies started voting, they also became candidates and many won elections. Three women have been elected governors of their states, Miriam "Ma" Ferguson of Texas, and Nellie Ross of Wyoming, in 1924, and Lurleen Wallace of Alabama in 1966. The Congress in 1965 included two lady Senators and 10 Congresswomen. More than 300 women serve in state legislatures and 10,000 women are in elected offices at the municipal level.

In the early days of the nation, almost all candidates for public office were white, Protestant, and of Anglo-Saxon heritage. Today candidates and public officials come from all races, religions, and ethnic backgrounds. A nation of immigrants in a land of opportunity now produces candidates with as much variety of race, creed, color, and national origin as is found among the American people.

Education, Wealth, and Occupation. Education has become an increasingly important characteristic of candidates. In this century, all but two Presidents were college graduates, as are the overwhelming majority of those now serving in Congress. Practically every candidate for every public office is a high school graduate.

Many candidates enjoy the advantage of personal wealth. Yet opportunities do exist for candidates without personal fortunes. Thousands of men and women of modest means, today, hold important offices in Washington and throughout the country.

Candidates come to politics from a variety of different jobs. Most candidates have had some experience in a minor governmental or political office before seeking higher office. Among the professions and jobs, the field of law produces more candidates than any other single occupation. Lawyers frequently find that their professional duties involve them in public issues, they learn to speak easily on their feet, their work often gets their names in the newspapers, and because they often work in association with other lawyers, they are able to take on part-time political positions without completely sacrificing their livelihood. More than half of the U. S. Senators and Congressmen in 1965 were lawyers (57%). This same Congress also included a large number of businessmen (27%) and a few teachers (9%) and newspapermen (7%).

Personal Characteristics. Most candidates were born or brought up in the communities in which they first seek political office. This is especially true for offices such as mayor, governor, Congressman, and U. S. Senator. Robert Kennedy's winning the Senate seat from New York in 1964—when he had not really lived there as an adult—is the exception that proves the rule. In the Western part of the country, however, where large numbers of people have moved into a state in recent years, there is a smaller political premium on native credentials. And throughout the country, political opportunities are still open to intelligent, aggressive men and women who make a new community their home after having grown up and completed their education elsewhere.

To generalize about the personalities of candidates is risky, for there is no mold in which to cast a successful candidate. Yet many candidates do have much in common. First and foremost, they are talkers. Confident and poised, they speak easily and fluently. An audience does not cause them stage fright; it brightens their eyes and gladdens their hearts! Endowed with that rare talent for stirring emotions, some excel before a large crowd. Others are most effective speaking informally to small groups in a living room. But almost all have the capacity—and the inclination—to talk often and effectively to audiences of any size.

Then, too, most candidates are good listeners. They have learned to learn from the voters, both for the information they acquire, and the favorable impression their listening creates.

They are generally at ease with all sorts of people. They are outgoing, gregarious, and fond of meeting and being with other people. With a few candidates, these traits are only skin-deep, as with the cartoonists' caricature of the "back-slapping glad-hander." But with candidates who wear well with the voters, this interest in people must be genuine. Insincerity is nowhere so easily exposed as in the glaring spotlight of politics.

Candidates usually pursue their interests in people by joining a variety of organizations within their communities. They become active in service clubs, veterans groups, religious and charitable organizations, and business, professional, labor, or farm clubs. These groups provide a wide potential of political support and also give the candidate an opportunity to compile a record of community service that will stand him in good stead with the voters.

Leadership.   A final characteristic is the intangible quality of leadership. Whatever traits of personality and character cause schoolmates to select a class president or a team captain often propel that person into political candidacy. It is not just popularity. People want candidates they can respect — men and women in whom they can place public trust. They want candidates with the capacity to look ahead, to point the way, to lead.

THE ROAD TO CANDIDACY

Seeking or Being Sought.   Most people who want to become candidates have to work at their ambition for a long time. Especially, if past elections indicate the nominee of one party has a good chance of winning, that nomination will be actively sought by many competitors. On the other hand, if one party's nominee has rarely if ever been elected, or if the opposition candidate is especially strong, the nomination may well go begging, and someone will have to be implored to enter the almost certainly hopeless contest. Occasionally, even when a nomination carries with it the likelihood of election, the party will seek out a person to be the candidate instead of the person seeking to become the candidate. In local and, sometimes, in state politics, the parties want a new, fresh personality, free of the scars and liabilities of past political battles. In just this fashion, Republican leaders in a California Congressional District, in 1946, asked a young Navy veteran to run for Congress. Six years later, Richard M. Nixon was elected Vice-President of the United States.

In national politics, the competition for nomination is so keen that the opportunity of being a candidate for President is rarely

Leading public figures are sometimes drafted as candidates outside of the party organization. Such a movement took place in 1964, when interested citizens won a write-in campaign for Henry Cabot Lodge in the New Hampshire primary.

thrust upon an unwilling person. The nearest modern example of a national party drafting a candidate was the 1952 Democratic National Convention's decision to nominate Adlai Stevenson for President.

Telling the Public.   Just because people want to be candidates does not necessarily mean that they always say so. In fact, one of the normal tactics in becoming a candidate is to steadfastly maintain that you do not intend to run. The theory is that this develops an appearance of modesty and an impression that the person ultimately runs only because of great popular demand. The denial is rarely genuine. In 1884, General Sherman found the words to convince his supporters that he positively was not a candidate for the Presidential nomination: "I will not accept if nominated and will not serve if elected." Any denial short of that ultimatum is readily discounted.

Perhaps the public today prefers to see men and women frankly acknowledge their interest in public office. John F. Kennedy in 1960 and Barry Goldwater in 1964 were officially off and running for a presidential nomination nearly a year before the election, and the open announcement of their objective seems to have been helpful to both.

Between outright seeking of office and feigned denial of interest lies the middle ground of quietly letting friends and political leaders know of your "availability." This technique preserves the public posture of modesty and, at the same time, encourages your supporters to help in winning the nomination.

Political Backgrounds. The best traveled route to major political candidacy runs from minor public office up through the higher reaches of state and national office. City and county officials have a good chance of becoming candidates for the state legislature. State representatives, state senators, mayors, and county district attorneys are often leading contenders for nomination to Congress. Most Congressmen are potential candidates for U. S. Senator. Candidates for President are almost always drawn from the ranks of governors or U. S. Senators.

Sometimes participation in the political process at the staff level leads to candidacy. Several men who have served as assistants to Senators and Congressmen have later returned to their home areas to run for office. Of these the most successful has been a one-time assistant to a Texas Congressman. In 1935, he left his boss, ran successfully on his own the following year, and became Congressman Lyndon B. Johnson.

Those in the political process as party leaders rarely become candidates. A person holding office within a political party, such as a county or state chairman, usually acquires a reputation for being too much the politician, a liability among voters. A notable exception in modern times was the Democratic party leader in Pennsylvania, David Lawrence, who became mayor of Pittsburgh and, later, governor of his state.

The role of campaign manager sometimes leads to a nomination because campaign activity provides close contact with party leaders throughout a state. In 1950, the manager of a successful campaign for governor of Arizona was Barry Goldwater. Two years later, he won nomination and election to the U. S. Senate.

A Well-known Name.   Apart from the progression of public offices, the best boost for candidacy comes from fame, becoming

United Press International Photo

Starting as a Congressman and a supporter of Franklin D. Roosevelt in 1937, Lyndon B. Johnson has since moved up the political ladder to President of the United States.

well and favorably known to the public. A man endowed with a well-known family name often has a big advantage. Modern examples are President Kennedy's brothers, Senators Robert and Edward Kennedy, and President Roosevelt's sons, former Congressmen Franklin D. Roosevelt, Jr., and James Roosevelt, and Miami Beach Mayor Elliott Roosevelt.

On the Republican side the names Taft, Lodge, and Rockefeller have proven to be major assets for aspiring candidates. President William Howard Taft's son became Senator Robert Taft, and the Senator's son became a Congressman and was the unsuccessful Republican candidate for Senator from Ohio in 1964. Henry Cabot Lodge, Jr., the grandson of the Senator who led the fight against the United States joining the League of Nations, also became a U. S. Senator and, later, the unsuccessful candidate for Vice-President in 1960. His son, George, became a candidate for U. S. Senator in 1962, losing to Senator Edward Kennedy. In 1966, two Rockefeller brothers were elected governor, Nelson Rockefeller for a third term in New York and Winthrop Rockefeller in an upset victory in Arkansas. At the same time their nephew, John D. Rockefeller IV, won a seat in the West Virginia state legislature as a Democrat. Name and family tie have been very helpful to the candidacy of several women who entered politics after the death of their politically active husbands. Two lady Senators, Maurine Neuberger of Oregon, who retired in 1966, and Margaret Chase Smith of Maine, who won a fourth term in 1966, first became successful candidates upon the death of their husbands, Senator Richard Neuberger and Congressman Clyde Smith.

A name often becomes well known in politics through a succession of defeats. William Proxmire ran three times for Governor of Wisconsin without success. But in the process, he became well enough known to win election to the U. S. Senate in 1958 and re-election in 1964. John Sherman Cooper, of Kentucky, has lost two Senate campaigns, but he has also won election to the Senate five times, for either full or part terms.

Efforts to gain political success from well-known names reached a peak in the Democratic primaries in Oklahoma in 1938. Contenders for various nominations included Daniel Boone, Joe E. Brown, Robert Burns, Patrick Henry, Sam Houston, John L. Lewis, Huey Long, Mae West, Wilbur Wright, Brigham Young, and four men named Will Rogers.

Will a name well known outside of government be a political asset? That is less certain. The 1964 elections provided mixed evidence. John Glenn, who gained fame as an astronaut, was considered a serious contender for the Democratic nomination for U. S. Senator from Ohio, until an unfortunate injury caused him to withdraw. Pierre Salinger, known to the public as President Kennedy's press secretary, won a hotly contested nomination for U. S. Senator from California, but lost the election to Republican George Murphy, known to the public primarily as a movie actor. In Oklahoma, the Republican nomination for Senator was won by Bud Wilkinson, a nationally known college football coach, but he lost the election. In 1966, Ronald Reagan's name and face were surely major assets in his successful campaign to become Governor of California.

The best nonpolitical source of politically useful fame has been military success. When General George Washington became the

Ronald Reagan's fame as a Hollywood motion picture star and television actor helped him along the road to victory over the incumbent in the 1966 gubernatorial race in California.

first President, he started a pattern that was to be followed by Andrew Jackson, William Henry Harrison, Zachary Taylor, Ulysses S. Grant and Dwight D. Eisenhower. All became President after acquiring national fame as military leaders.

Without the headstart of a well-known name, the aspiring candidate works within his community to bring himself to public attention. Participation in civic and charitable activities often provides opportunities to serve the public and to come to the attention of the people. Here, the would-be candidate has a chance to show that he is useful, to make an occasional speech, and to have his name mentioned in the newspapers. That combination supplies a big boost along the road to candidacy.

Timing and Luck. Affecting all efforts to become a candidate are the uncontrollable factors of timing and just plain luck. One year, for example, the party decides to run a certain type of candidate. That choice is based in part on the opposition candidate, the rest of the ticket, the issues of the year, the results of past elections, and the educated guesses about the outcome of future elections. Once that choice is made, those who fit the bill are in the running; those who don't, have long odds against them before they begin. "This just isn't your year," is the stock answer hundreds of political leaders have given to thousands of aspirants who sought a nomination.

If it just happens to be the year when a certain person is exactly what the political leaders want, that man or woman is on the way to becoming a candidate and perhaps entering a long career in public office. If the circumstances of that year cause the politicians to look elsewhere, his career will most likely not start that year and perhaps never at all.

This is not to suggest that a capable, ambitious person cannot swim upstream against strong political currents. It has been done and will be done again and again. Those who do it successfully will be interviewed at the height of a political career, and the reporters will dutifully record that "Congressman Jones" set his sights on elective office at the age of 8 and pursued his goal relentlessly ever since. No doubt he did. But it is equally true, and less often reported, that thousands of others of equal ability also wanted to become candidates and never made it at all.

In many cases the difference between becoming a candidate and winning, or forever remaining a hopeful, is just luck. In 1964, scores of promising Republican candidates lost, and many Democrats won unexpected victories for the simple reason that they happened to be running the year Lyndon Johnson overwhelmed Barry Goldwater.

Sometimes good luck is not always recognizable, as a personal example will show. In 1952, Abe Ribicoff, of Connecticut, ran as the Democratic candidate for an unexpired four-year term in the U. S. Senate—and lost. Had he won, he would have faced likely defeat in 1956, because Eisenhower's victory was large enough in Connecticut to elect all seven Republican candidates for the Senate and the House. That might well have ended his political career. But in the 1952 loss Ribicoff made a good enough showing to merit the nomination for Governor two years later. Elected in 1954 for a four-year term as Governor, he survived the 1956 Republican surge in Connecticut because he did not have to run that year. Thereafter, he won re-election as Governor and went on to President Kennedy's Cabinet and election to the U. S. Senate.

WHY CANDIDATES RUN

How many applicants would you expect to answer the following want-ad?

> WANTED—male or female for frustrating job. SALARY —less than you presently make. HOURS—long with no payments for overtime. ADVANCEMENT—highly unpredictable. SECURITY—none whatever. WORKING CONDITIONS— subject to constant harassment by members of the public, often at any hour of the day or night.

Not many? Yet this description of elective office attracts thousands of candidates every year, with many thousands more lined up waiting for a chance to apply. Despite the headaches of public office and the heartaches of a losing campaign, the allure of politics grows stronger by the year.

Why do they run? There are many reasons, some noble, some not. None applies to all candidates, but many apply to most of them.

Public Service. Most candidates run to have a say in public affairs. Whether the issue is city traffic, state funds for education, or peace in the world, candidates go one step further than the average citizen. They not only have opinions on what should be done, they want the chance to put those opinions to work. Many citizens have a chance to affect public affairs in their private roles. Businessmen and labor leaders have an impact on the economy, on wages, prices, and profits. Professional men and women have a major voice in matters concerning their fields, whether law, medicine, education, or others. Civic and charitable groups shape public policy in many areas affecting human welfare. But the governmental role is more active, more direct, and often more decisive.

Many an exasperated citizen, concerned with public issues, has thrown up his hands in despair and proclaimed, "There ought to be a law!" Candidates take that next step and seek positions where they can do something to get the law passed.

For most candidates the attraction of public life is the opportunity to feel useful—an opportunity equalled in few other endeavors. Most men and women see a usefulness in whatever job they hold. Many find the need to augment their usefulness by civic and charitable activity that benefits their communities. But public life holds out the challenge of constant participation in the affairs of community, state, and nation. Just participating provides tremendous satisfaction. Often, there is the added stimulation of affecting the outcome, of leaving your thumbprints on the solution to a vexing public problem.

Power, Fame, and Fortune. Some candidates enter the political arena drawn by the lure of power. In few other human activities can you gain so much power so quickly. For many this is but a means to the end of accomplishing constructive results. But for a few men in public life the exercise of power is an end in itself. They would find it difficult to explain what they are trying to accomplish. For them, politics is a game where the winner has power, and the object is simply to hold power as long as possible.

Nearly all candidates are motivated, to some extent, by the desire for fame. Only the worlds of entertainment and sports rival politics for the abundance of fame that can quickly descend upon the successful. Anyone who has ever been pleased to see his name in print (and who hasn't?) naturally enjoys the spotlight of politics. It's not just the publicity. It's the special thrill of public acceptance, sometimes even acclaim. The thundering applause of an admiring audience, once heard, will be pursued by many for a lifetime.

Fame and fortune often go hand in hand but not necessarily in politics. Many officeholders are paid far less than they would earn in nonpolitical jobs. And many part-time officeholders, like city councilmen, find that the demands of their office cut down the time available for their private occupations. But some candidates do enter politics, in part at least, because of the hope of financial reward. It is not just the salary of the office that counts, although public salaries have increased rapidly in recent years. More often they believe that their new political fame will increase their private earning capacity. A struggling young lawyer, forbidden by the ethics of his profession from advertising for clients, often find politics the best way to make his name known to his community. Then, there are always a very few individuals who see politics as a chance to use public power for private again. Often illegal and always unethical, such activity occurs less and less in modern politics, but even isolated examples must not be tolerated.

Just Plain Fun. One motivation surely common to all candidates is the undeniable fact that politics is fun. It is variety and adventure and excitement. It is unpredictable. It is a trade practiced by some of the most entertaining people in the land. They enjoy humor, and they find humor in the oddities and absurdities of political life. Members of all professions like to talk shop. So do politicians, but with this difference. Where lawyers or doctors will harangue each other with serious discussions of their cases, politicians would rather swap anecdotes from the rich and often comical history of politics. It is a calling of colorful figures who live life to the fullest and enjoy every minute of it. They will complain and tell you it's hard work with many bruises to the ego and blows to morale. But they genuinely like what they are doing and will not willingly quit.

The Political Bug. Candidates run for all of these reasons and for the inexplicable reason that the bite of the political bug causes a disease that lasts a lifetime. The exposure may occur anywhere — doing menial chores in the campaign headquarters of a candidate for major office, sharing a candidate's victory celebration on election night, ringing doorbells and making your first political pitch to a voter, or just standing in the crowd as a Presidential nominee rides triumphantly through town, or listening when a local candidate makes a stirring speech.

From the first exposure the disease takes firm hold. You devote your time, your energy, and your talents. An election campaign ends, and you start thinking about the next one. You know that everyone cannot be a candidate, but soon you begin to believe that you have as good a chance as the next person — maybe better. From that point on, there is no known cure. You have left the grandstand and become an active participant. And if you are like most of those who have gone before, you will stay with politics for the rest of your life.

4

POLITICAL PARTIES

Almost all candidates and most voters are members of a political party. Yet the idea of "party" has many different meanings for both candidates and voters.

To a candidate, "party" may be the handful of local leaders who can give or deny him a nomination, or the thousands of people whose vote he can count on because he and they share the same party label, or the policies he favors which were advocated by Presidents and Senators of his party in the past.

For the voter, "party" may mean a family tradition of political allegiance extending back four generations, or a local political club whose members are bound more in friendship than political philosophy, or just a label opposite his name on a voter-registration list to be followed or disregarded depending on who is running. The voter may think of a party as a meaningful instrument for taking sides on the great public issues of his day, or an organization to which he contributes $100 a year and a few hours of work each fall, or an informal designation he freely acknowledges but firmly believes has absolutely no meaning at all.

Still, the concept of "party"—for all its various meanings—is at the heart of American politics. About 75 million American voters consider themselves Republicans or Democrats. The President, every Governor, every Senator, every Representative, and almost every state legislator and mayor are members of either the Republican or Democratic Parties. They were nominated by their parties and won, in the aggregate, millions of votes from people who were ready to vote for anyone running under their party's banner.

For all its importance in our political system, this party tradition was not established as part of the system of government when our nation was formed. While the Constitution is very specific in providing for much of our political machinery, especially the method of electing the President and members of the national legislature, it says not a single word about political parties. The fact is that many of the men who founded this country did not expect political parties to develop, certainly not the broadly-based party organizations that dominate our political life today. In his Farewell Address, George Washington warned of the "baneful effects of the spirit of party generally."

THEORY AND PURPOSE OF PARTIES

Ideas and Action. A political party is a group of people who have in common some general ideas of public policy and a very specific idea of political action—that members of their group should be elected to public office. This double concern for ideas and action runs through the formation, organization, and operation of parties. It explains much of what holds parties together, how they are able to maintain the support of individuals of widely different backgrounds, viewpoints, and objectives.

People who are interested in ideas—especially ideas about what should be done in their community, state, and nation—are aware that those in public office are in the best position to get things done. So the thinkers seek out the doers and make common cause with them to translate thought into action. For their part, those who seek the many satisfactions of public office know that success depends in large part on the quality and strength of their philosophy. So they join with people who can contribute to or, at least, support the points of view they find agreeable. A bond of thought and action develops—an alliance of people with ideas, people who share these ideas, and people who want to see to it that their government acts upon these ideas. All find their place in a political party.

Many groups in our society have the first ingredient of ideas they wish to advance. Our business, labor, farm, civic, professional, fraternal, nationality, and religious groups not only have some philosophy but also take some steps toward action. Some even move into political activity by supporting or opposing men for public office.

But only the political parties combine ideas with direct political action. The parties have a point of view, a collection of ideas, plans, and objectives, and they seek to nominate and elect people who represent their thinking. When manufacturers or doctors or farmers or labor organizations decide to back a political candidate, they do so primarily because they approve of his views, not because he is the representative of their group, nominated by them as their spokesman. But when the Republican or Democratic Parties nominate and support a candidate, they are selecting and backing him in his capacity as a representative of their group.

Normally, a political party is a broadly-based group including people of all occupations and backgrounds. But a group of farmers, for example, could decide they wanted a farmer to be in a position to take some governmental action. They could become a political party — a farmers' party, nominate their own candidate as a representative of their group, and try to get him elected.

Legal Requirements. These ingredients of party — philosophy and direct political action — are supplemented in this country by legal requirements. In most of our states, a political party must have a minimum number of members or meet with minimum success at the polls before it can claim to be an official party. These minimum requirements determine when a party is entitled to have its candidates appear on the ballot at election time. Some state laws require a petition signed by 1% of the state's voters for the party to get a place on the ballot the first time; thereafter, the new party must win at least the same percent of votes in order to remain on the ballot at future elections. Some states have tried to discourage third parties by extending places on the ballot only to parties that win a sizable share of the total vote.

The states began to adopt these legal requirements at the end of the 19th century. The cause was the first use of official ballots printed by many states, which listed party candidates. Once a state gave status to parties by placing their candidates on an official ballot, rules became necessary to determine when a group was entitled to be considered a party.

Why Parties Develop. There are many theories about why parties are formed. The simplest maintains that in all matters of public policy there is bound to be more than one point of view. Once one position gains adherents, those who think otherwise will want to organize to give voice to their differing view. Sometimes the difference centers mainly on one issue—as when the Prohibition Party was formed to ban the sale and drinking of alcoholic beverages. Usually political parties are formed on broader viewpoints. They may represent a difference between philosophies—whether, in general, past traditions should be preserved or whether changes should be made. The difference may be economic—whether government policy should favor the interests of employers or the interests of workers. Or the difference may concern an attitude toward government itself—whether government should take an active role to improve conditions in society or whether government should keep its role to a minimum with private activity making most needed improvements. Or the interests of one part of a country with seaports and factories may be opposed to the interests of another part where farming is dominant. In some countries, parties are formed, or at least maintained, by the common interests of one nationality or religious group. This has not been the pattern in the United States.

Political parties often are formed from several groups which find they can best advance their separate points of view by joining together. All members of the party will not feel as strongly as others about all issues on which the party takes a stand. Some members may even be opposed to the stand of the party on matters of relative unimportance. But they all find it advantageous to stay together so that when an election is won, most of the members find most of their views being advanced by the elected members of their party.

Once formed, political parties tend to stay in existence a long time, especially those that have won enough support to be considered major parties. Issues may arise on which the members sharply disagree, but they make an effort to live with their differences, knowing that their unity will help them to make progress in those areas where they are in substantial agreement. Moreover, parties tend to stay responsive to new viewpoints that have the support of large numbers of voters. Most parties temper their previous positions to keep up with the public, rather than cling to unpopular positions and forfeit any chance for success at the polls.

There are parties, however, that adhere to a position regardless of the lack of broad popular support. The Socialist Labor Party and the Socialist Workers Party run candidates for President and some other offices pledged to governmental policies completely unacceptable to all but a handful of American voters.

THE AMERICAN TWO-PARTY SYSTEM

The most significant fact about the system of political parties in the United States has been the existence of two major parties rather than the half a dozen or more found in other countries.

Why Two Parties?   Why we have just two major parties is not clear. One reason may be the rules of our elections. First, the most important person in our government, the President, is elected by the votes of all the people through their vote, in each state, for members of the electoral college. A majority vote of the electoral college is necessary to elect the President.[1] In that kind of election only two parties could hope to have much chance of winning. Throughout our history, no third party has ever succeeded in winning the presidency. The major attempts have been those by the Progressive Party. In 1912, its first candidate, Theodore Roosevelt, won 27% of the popular vote and 88 electoral votes. In 1924, the Progressive candidate, Robert LaFollette, won 16% of the popular vote but just 13 electoral votes.

Secondly, our legislators run for election in single-member districts. Since only one Congressman is elected in each district, it is difficult for a third party to have a serious chance of success against the candidates of the two major parties. In other countries, where several members are elected from each district, the vote of a

---

[1] In the unlikely event that no presidential candidate wins a majority of the electoral college, the House of Representatives (with each state's delegation casting a single vote) selects a President from among the three candidates receiving the most votes in the electoral college. This has happened only twice in our history — in 1800, when Thomas Jefferson was elected under this procedure, and in 1824, when the winner was John Quincy Adams.

third party may be large enough to elect one or two people, though far short of a plurality of all the votes cast.

Aside from these procedural reasons, the stability of our two-party system is perhaps influenced by the absence of sharply divisive issues within the country. There is a broad consensus within the country on many issues, and two parties seem to provide enough dispute for most peoples' tastes. If, for example, many people wanted to make radical changes, such as altering our form of government, they would have to form a third party to express such a position. This could not be done within the framework of our existing parties. Indeed, when this country faced its most serious internal conflict over the issue of slavery, one result was the creation of a new political party. The northern wing of the Whig Party found it could not satisfactorily oppose slavery and stay within the party. This group left the Whigs and became the core of the new Republican Party.

Finally, our two-party system seems to rest in large part on its acceptance by nearly all the people of this country. We like it, we are used to it, and we are therefore reluctant to experiment with efforts to change the system.

Start of the Two-Party System.   The two-party system began in this country almost with the formation of the Union and has continued virtually uninterrupted to the present. While on occasion parties have disappeared and others have been formed to take their places, a fairly continuous pattern emerges in which the economic and sectional groups that were identified with our original parties are still roughly identified with the present-day successors of those early parties.

The formation of our country split the populace into the Federalists, who supported creation of a central government with strong powers, and the anti-Federalists, who if not all opposed to formation of a new government, at least preferred that it have only very limited power. The core of the Federalist strength was the bankers, manufacturers, and businessmen from the coastal areas, while the main Anti-Federalist strength came from the farmers in the inland areas. The initial government of President George Washington was controlled by the Federalists. Under the leadership of Thomas Jefferson, a political party known both as Republican and

Democratic-Republican was formed, largely from the ranks of the former Anti-Federalists. Jefferson's party took an active role in the election of 1792, agreeing to Washington's re-election, but trying, unsuccessfully, to win the Vice-Presidency.

The Democratic-Republicans came to power with Jefferson's election as President in 1800. The party had grown to include many Northern workingmen and Southern landowners. Meanwhile, the power of the Federalists dwindled. Even some of its support from businessmen was lost to Jefferson's party, and its reactionary stance during the War of 1812 cost it further strength. The Federalist Party came to an end as an effective national force in 1816.

Four years later, President James Monroe was re-elected, virtually without party opposition, in a period historians have called "The Era of Good Feeling." But the success of the Democratic-Republicans led to in-fighting within the party. The election of 1824 saw four members of the party all receiving electoral votes for President, with the result that none won a majority, and the House of Representatives chose John Quincy Adams. This fight split the Democratic-Republicans. Under the leadership of Andrew Jackson, one wing styled itself the Democratic Party and went on to win the Presidency for Jackson in 1828 and 1832. The other wing, known as the National Republicans joined with others in 1834 to form a united opposition to the Democrats under the label of the Whig Party. Both in geography and economic interests, the new party strongly resembled the Federalists. Jackson's Democratic Party traced its lineage back to Jefferson's Democratic-Republicans and to the Anti-Federalists before them. For 20 years after 1836, control shifted back and forth between the Whigs and the Democrats.

The slavery issue caused an upheaval in politics as in all of the nation's life. In 1854, the Whigs split disastrously on the issue and came to an end as a party. The Northern Whigs joined with small farmers from the ranks of the Democrats to form, in 1856, the Republican Party, and chose Colonel John C. Fremont as their presidential candidate. Their first presidential victory came with Abraham Lincoln in 1860. The Democrats continued as a party but Northern defections weakened their power and they failed to win back the presidency until 1884.

After the Civil War.   The Republicans remained the dominant party from the Civil War until 1932, yielding only to the Democratic victories of Grover Cleveland in 1884 and 1892 and Woodrow Wilson in 1912 and 1916. Throughout this period, the Republicans drew their strength heavily from the East and Midwest, from the wealthy and the prospering middle classes. The Democrats, while maintaining some strength in all parts of the country, were strongest in the South and with the poorer classes, especially those in the Northern cities. Wilson's election in 1912 not only provided victory for the Democrats but laid the foundation for the party's future strength. In the 1912 campaign, Teddy Roosevelt led those dissatisfied with Taft and the Republicans into the Progressive Party. Voters concerned with issues like conservation and governmental reform stayed with this third party for a time, but many of them, once isolated from the Republicans, never returned and ultimately found a new home with the Democrats.

After eight years of Wilson, the Republicans were overwhelmingly returned to power and remained in control of the White House for the next 12 years. Then dismay at the Great Depression, the growth of Democratic strength in the cities, and the personal appeal of Franklin D. Roosevelt brought about a decisive end to Republican control in 1932.

Roosevelt's victory in that year marked a basic shift in the position of the Democrats from minority to majority status that has continued until the present except for the Eisenhower victories in 1952 and 1956. From 1932 to 1966 Democrats have won control of the House of Representatives in each biannual election except 1946 and 1952.

Modern National Parties. Both major parties, today, include a broad representation of almost all groups within our country. If any one factor tends to identify the adherents of the parties, it is most likely to be income. By and large, most of the middle class and the wealthy are Republicans and most of the low-income and poor families are Democrats. There is no uniformity, however, and you can find plenty of rich Democrats and poor Republicans! The geographical patterns of the past can still be observed, though they are changing. Republicans draw their strength from parts of the Northeast, the Midwest, and the Rocky Mountain states. Democrats win regularly in much of the South and in the cities of the

James J. Dobbins, *The Boston Herald Traveler*

North. In fact, the increase in the size of city populations has been one of the main reasons why the Democratic Party has become the majority party.

The South has been an exception to the normal workings of two-party politics. The Democrats have so completely dominated party politics there that until very recently no serious Republican opposition arose. Republicans failed even to nominate candidates for most state offices and for Congress. Since the Democratic nominees were assured of election, the only serious contests were waged within the Democratic Party for nominations.

In recent years, however, Republican activity has revived in the South, especially in the cities. Eisenhower, Nixon, and Goldwater each captured the electoral votes of Southern states in their presidential campaigns, and since 1960, several Republican candidates in Southern states have been elected to Congress and to state legislatures. In 1966, Republicans elected governors in Arkansas and Florida, re-elected Senator John Tower in Texas, and elected Congressmen throughout the South.

State Party Patterns. The two-party pattern of national politics is not necessarily repeated within all of the states. In perhaps a third of the states, the strength of the two major parties is roughly even, and competition between them parallels the national pattern. But in most states one party or the other dominates the political scene. While the opposition party is active, it has only an outside chance of winning the governorship and, in some instances, virtually no chance at all of winning control of the state legislature. That is the normal prospect facing Democrats in South Dakota and Republicans in Georgia.

Where one party is dominant, three patterns of party conflict result. Sometimes the major party divides into two factions that oppose each other like full-fledged parties in a two-party state. Each faction supports candidates in the party primary, and that battle is the decisive election in the state. The factions maintain their identity and support from year to year. Louisiana follows this pattern to a large extent.

In other states, factionalism breaks out within the dominant party, but follows no continuous pattern. The primary is still the key election, but the contending forces form their ranks for each battle behind new candidates, and little identity can be observed between the factions from one year to the next. That is usually the pattern of state contests in Texas and Florida.

In a few states where one party is dominant, the lesser party is still strong enough to have a chance at control whenever factionalism splits the strength of the major party. Republican victories in Kentucky and Democratic victories in New Hampshire have resulted from this pattern.

Party Control in State Legislatures. Even where the two parties battle on even terms in statewide elections for presidential electors, Governors, and Senators, one party often maintains control of one house of the state legislature. This has occurred most frequently in Northern states where Democrats often win governorships but find Republicans in control of the lower house of the legislature. In Connecticut, for example, both parties compete on even terms for all statewide offices with roughly equal success.

Yet 1958 was the first time since 1876 that Democrats won both houses of the state legislature. New Jersey Democrats won both houses in 1965 for the first time since 1912. Republican control of these Northern legislatures has been aided by the system of representation. Until recently the common pattern was to have members of one house represent approximately equal numbers of people, and members of the other house represent geographical units such as counties or towns. There would always be a larger number of rural counties than city counties; so the party that did best in the rural areas – the Republicans – was assured of winning more seats than the Democrats in the legislative house based on geography. Whichever party won the governorship, however, had won a majority of the population and thereby won a majority of the members of the house in which representation was based on population.

In 1962, the United States Supreme Court ruled that the Constitution requires seats in both houses of a state legislature to be based on equal numbers of people. This ruling forces reapportionment of those state legislatures where representation was based on counties or towns, regardless of how few people lived in them. Once both houses are reapportioned on the basis of population, the result will usually be that the party that wins the majority needed to elect a Governor will also elect a majority of both houses of the legislature. This opportunity for clear-cut control of the executive and legislative branches by the victorious party in state elections is the most significant development in state party politics in this century.

PARTISAN POLITICS

A favorite criticism of the American party system is that there are few if any clear points of difference between the two major parties. It is true that American parties are not tightly disciplined organizations in which all of the members of one party think one way on any given issue and all members of the other party think the other way. Both major parties include within their ranks people with all sorts of views on all sorts of issues. There is, however, a consensus within each party on many issues, and the consensus of one party often differs from the other's in philosophy and in specific results.

Basic Differences Between the Parties. An essential difference stems understandably from a basic difference in the parties' sources of strength. Gaining large support from the middle classes and the wealthy, some Republicans are generally inclined to support the interests of manufacturing and commercial enterprises. Many Democrats, aware of their support from the ranks of the lower income and the poor, tend to favor the interests of working people and the disadvantaged. This distinction must not be overdrawn. As a party, Republicans often act in the best interests of low-income families, and Democrats often support measures to assist business interests. Then, too, this distinction along economic lines must recognize the differing views within the parties. A few Republican Senators like Clifford Case of New Jersey and Jacob Javits of New York take more advanced social welfare positions than many Democrats. And a few Southern Democrats are less progressive than many Republicans. But even with these allowances, the difference in emphasis between the parties on economic issues persists.

This difference has led, especially since 1932, to a shift in the parties' traditional view of the proper role of Federal governmental power. The Federalists of the 1790's, forerunners of today's Republicans, used the National Government to help business interests. For example, high duties were set on imported products to protect American manufacturers from foreign competition. And Congress passed laws to strengthen the position of wealthy creditors. But such measures worked against the interests of those who owed money, many of whom were supporters of Jefferson's early Democratic Party. Seeing Federal power used in these ways, the forerunners of today's Democrats tended to distrust it.

In modern America, however, the power of the Federal government has on some occasions come to be used against large business interests, as in the antitrust field, and in favor of the interests of the workingmen and the poor. As a result, Democrats now find that the interests they want to see advanced are often aided by further activity of the Federal government, which they now support.

Republicans now find their interests are best served by minimizing the role of the Federal government.

Of course, Democrats do not advocate having the Federal government solve all of America's problems, and Republicans do not oppose all Federal programs. But when it is suggested that a Federal law be passed to deal with some new problem, the chances are that most Democrats will support it. Most Republicans will either oppose it or at least suggest an alternative approach under which Federal power is reduced, and state power or private resources are given a larger role. Recent battles over medical care for the aged and aid to education illustrate these trends.

Both parties tend to place different interpretations on their approaches to both economics and Federal governmental power. The Democrats emphasize their concern for people of modest means, and minimize, and even deny, their reliance on Federal power. On the other hand, Republicans minimize, and even deny, their support of business interests, but put great stress on their philosophy of government. They believe greater reliance on state and local government and private initiative leads to increased individual freedom, which, they say, is threatened by expanding Federal power. The Democrats respond that the economic and social policies which they pursue through the use of Federal power expand individual opportunities and in this way lead to increased individual freedom.

Though these differences in basic approach exist, the parties themselves often tend to blur the differences rather than sharpen them. The reason for this lies in the deep tradition of the two-party system. Both parties know that a third party has little chance of gaining substantial strength. The battle in the next election is sure to be between the two parties now in existence. Knowing this, each party feels confident that it can move to the middle ground without serious fear of losing the support of its extreme members. And both parties can see that in a closely divided two-party system, victory will go to the party that can occupy the middle ground. So neither party goes out of its way to emphasize its differences with the other; both prefer to present to the public a claim that they can each satisfy the wishes of a sizable majority of the public.

Party Responsibility.   The blurring of party differences is a disappointment to those political scientists who believe that democracy functions best when voters are confronted with clear-cut choices at election time. They argue that only if the parties are clearly identified with opposing positions on public issues can the voters intelligently express their views on these issues. What they really want is more than just differences between party positions. They would like the elected officials of both parties, especially in the state and Federal legislatures, to be required to give consistent support to party positions with their votes on legislation. They prefer a system of "party responsibility" under which legislators will support their party's position even though it conflicts with their personal judgment. To a large extent that system prevails in the British Parliament.

The absence of such a system in the U. S. Congress is explained not so much by the lack of differences between parties as by the limited ability of our parties to require legislators to support their party's positions. In England, the party has a firm hold on its members in Parliament. There, the party's ultimate weapon is the power to deny a member renomination. If a member fails to support the party's position on important issues, the national party will see to it that someone else is nominated from his district. A member thus disciplined usually has no effective way to win a nomination in his district, or any other, in the face of party opposition.

In this country, however, the national parties have virtually no say in state and local nominations for seats in Congress. States' rights clearly prevail in politics. Nominations are determined exclusively within the states; often, state political parties are powerless to influence nominations in Congressional Districts within the states. Even when a party has control of the White House and has as vigorous a President as Franklin D. Roosevelt, recalcitrant party members who vote against the party's position cannot be denied renomination. Roosevelt tried, in 1938, to engineer the defeat of several Democratic lawmakers who had opposed him. He was almost completely unsuccessful.

Knowing that the national party cannot effectively discipline him to the extent of denying him renomination, the legislator in the U. S. Congress casts his votes on the basis of what he thinks is right and what he thinks is wanted by his constituents. The voters who send a Democrat to Congress from Georgia do not necessarily agree with the voters who send a Democrat from California. Nor do the voters who send a Republican to Congress from Iowa necessarily agree with the voters who send a Republican from New York. With the membership of both major parties spread across a huge country, and lawmakers responsive to local constituencies, it is not surprising that at least at the national level we lack strict party responsibility.

Partisanship in Congress. There is, however, a cohesion among party members in Congress, and the national party leaderships can exert some influence on their members to support party positions. Democrats and Republicans in Congress often stick together unless the issue before them is one of compelling personal or local importance. Party loyalty can be influenced most effectively by the party in power at the White House. The President's power to name people to important positions, his power to endorse or oppose Federal projects in a lawmaker's home area, and his power over the fate of bills of special interest to an individual Senator or Congressman enable him to persuade most members of his party to support his side of an issue most of the time. The opposition party must seek unity without this power. Both party leaderships seek to compel party loyalty by offering promises of help at election time. Campaign funds are distributed by Senate and House campaign committees of both parties, and a recalcitrant party member can look forward to little or no help from these sources.

The 1964 election produced one of the few instances in our history where clear-cut party disloyalty was punished by party action within Congress. Two Democratic Congressmen who actively supported the Republican presidential candidate were denied their seniority on congressional committees and placed at the most junior positions. This punitive action was taken by the Democratic members of the House. One of the Congressmen thus censured resigned from the Democratic Party and from Congress, became a Republican, and was promptly re-elected to his former seat.

Despite many differences of opinion within parties at the national level, Congressional members almost invariably remain as members of their party. Even those Southern Democrats and Northern

Republicans who frequently vote with the opposition party in Congress find it helpful to stay with their own party when the time comes for winning renomination and re-election. In recent years, the only Senators who have formally changed parties are Wayne Morse of Oregon, who became a Democrat in 1954, and J. Strom Thurmond of South Carolina, who became a Republican in 1964.

Political Realignment. One proposal frequently made to sharpen the difference between the national parties is political realignment. All the liberal legislators in the Republican Party would join the Democratic Party, and all the conservative Democrats would switch over to the Republicans. The result would be two new parties, each with a more consistent political philosophy. Whichever party won control of Congress could be expected to line up the votes of nearly all its members in the Senate and House in support of the party's position on major issues. Such re-aligned parties would give the voters a more distinct choice between political viewpoints.

However, the proposal runs the risk of causing a splintering of the major parties. If each party has a somewhat unified position, differences are likely to break out within the parties. The result might then be the formation of several parties, each representing a portion of political thought along the spectrum from conservative to liberal. This would complicate the choice facing the voters and very likely weaken the effectiveness of Congress.

State and Local Partisanship. At the state level, party affiliation in legislatures often has greater significance than in Congress. In some states, it is not unusual for most of the votes in the state legislature to be cast on a strict party-line basis. Such discipline occurs in those states where a strong party organization has considerable power over the nomination of state senators and representatives and over their advancement to positions of influence within the legislature and within the party. Generally, the absence of regional differences makes it easier for members of one party in a state legislature to join together on most issues.

At the local level of government, the trend in this country in recent years has been away from partisan politics toward a system of nonpartisan elections and government. The argument has been made that there is no Democratic or Republican way to run a fire department or a garbage collection system; therefore, the handling of these tasks should be removed from partisan conflict and left to professional city administrators. In many cities which have abandoned partisan elections, city affairs are run by a professionally trained city manager, and policy matters are left to a city council whose members are elected without regard to party labels.

Even in the larger cities that have retained partisan elections, the strength of the parties has been diminished by the development of needed civic reforms. For example, 50 years ago the mayor of a large city could appoint several hundred party members to city jobs as reward for work done and as incentive for future party loyalty. With civil service systems in widespread use today, nearly all such jobs now go to applicants strictly on the basis of merit. The positions are filled by better qualified people, but the parties have lost one of the means by which they were able to maintain strength as parties.

The Paradox of Partisan Politics.   Party politics has been caught in an inevitable conflict between those who want "good government" and those who want "party responsibility." As reforms such as civil service have taken hold, the quality of government has been greatly improved. But this very trend has taken from the parties their power to compel party allegiance by elected representatives. A weak party finds it difficult, if not impossible, to gain a party-line vote for measures in a state or National legislature. Yet many people believe that an increase in party-line voting is desirable because it makes public issues clearer to the voters and offers them meaningful choices between those who run on the tickets of the major parties.

In essence, political parties are frequently criticized for being so political, yet they are expected to operate effectively in a governmental system that is political. For politics—at its best—is simply the means by which the wishes of the public are translated into governmental action. Democracy requires politics, and politics requires vigorous, competitive political parties.

5

THE
GOVERNMENT
OF
POLITICS

Politics is the system that helps national, state, and local governments to function, yet politics itself has its own internal system of government. Within each of the major political parties is a somewhat private governmental structure similar to the public system of government. Paralleling elections to public offices are elections within the parties, for positions of party leadership. Just as with public government, citizens have rights and public officials have powers, in political parties, too, there are rights of party members and powers of party leaders. The parties have constitutions, harmonious transfers of power, civil wars, and, occasionally, revolutions.

As with most systems of government, politics has wise leaders and ineffective leaders; honest officials and some corrupt ones. It has hotly-contested party elections and many that go by default for lack of opposition. Sometimes the citizen-members of the government of politics are active and alert; other times they are lazy and indifferent.

The rules, traditions, and practices of party governments are as varied as the state and local governments in which they operate. There are differences from one state to another and differences within each state from one community or region to another.

What some party organizations consider normal operating procedures, others would consider outrageous. In some, a top official has real power; in others, he does little more than give advice which is not often followed. A county chairman in one state may have almost a free hand in naming his party's candidate for Congress. In another state, a county chairman may have virtually no influence upon party nominations. Party membership may mean the exclusive right to vote in party primaries in one state; in another there may be no such thing as official party membership. Even within one state or one area within a state, the pattern of operation of each of the major parties may be entirely different. More often, both parties function in much the same way in the same locale.

The variety of party government follows the variety of public government. The Governor of New York, whoever he happened to be, would in all likelihood not be able to get elected Governor of Kansas; and if he had the job in Kansas, he would find entirely different patterns of government than he was used to in New York. By the same token, party leaders in New York, if transplanted, would not be likely to occupy the same positions in Kansas, and even if they had the jobs, they would know little about the best way to get their jobs done.

FORMAL STRUCTURE

The structure of government within the parties follows a pattern similar to the structure of public government. There are local, county, state, and national levels of power. In our structure of public government, power increases from the lowest level to the highest, with the power of the President far greater than the power of Governors, and the Congress exercising more power than the state legislatures. In the government of politics, however, the state level of power is usually the most important. While there is a pyramid of party offices from the local to the national level, men and women who occupy the key positions at the state level, and in some states at the city or county level, have the major say in political affairs. Within the President's party, major party power is exercised by the President himself. But even he may find that some state and county political leaders often have more power than he has in dealing with party matters.

The state level in the government of politics becomes important because that is where the key party decisions are made—who gets nominated, and who controls the party machinery. Rarely can a party official from the national level influence the selection of a candidate for public office in one of the states. Nor can he affect the choice of state and local party leaders. A party's national chairman might on occasion try to conciliate disputes between rival factions within a state party organization, but he will rarely try to dictate the terms of settlement. Even when the time comes to make the ultimate party decision of national significance—the selection of a presidential candidate—state party leaders, and some strong city and county chieftains, have the major influence.

Party Members. The "citizens" of the government of politics are the members of the political parties. A political party is one of the easiest organizations to join. There are no tests, no dues, and no need for sponsors or approval by a membership committee. Any voter is eligible. In some states he may become a party member at the time he registers to vote in a general election, simply by stating that he wishes to join a party. He is then formally listed as a party member and retains that party designation until he chooses to make a change.

In other states the time for choosing a party comes when a voter decides he wants to vote in a party primary to select candidates for public office. Some states that use the primary system require a voter to give some indication of party allegiance before permitting him to vote in a party primary. In these states a voter "joins" a party by giving election officials assurance of either his past, present, or future support of the party's candidates. Such assurance is largely a matter of the voter's own conscience. No one violates the secrecy of the voting booth to see which party's candidates the voter really supports.

Many states make no provision for formal party membership. Voters who want to participate in party activities simply show up at party meetings and speak out and vote on party matters.

Party members usually have the right to elect men and women to offices within the party structure. In some states, those who are not members have no say in the conduct of party affairs. They can vote in the elections for public office after the party candidates have been nominated, but they have no vote in the many primaries that are held to select party candidates for public office, and absolutely no vote or voice in the selection of party leaders. Membership in a political party, either formal or informal, is a requirement for full participation in political life.

The Precinct.   Both major parties are organized into political structures whose base is the precinct. This area of a few square blocks in a city, or a few square miles in a rural area, usually contains between 400 and 2,000 voters. There are more than 150,000 precincts in the United States. In some parts of the country precincts are called election districts, divisions, or blocks.

In some areas, especially in the cities, the precinct is simply a small subdivision of what may be called a ward, an election district, or an assembly district. These units, the wards and districts, or sometimes the precincts themselves, are the important units at the grass roots level. They function as units within the political structure, the leaders are usually chosen by party members who reside in the district, and their leadership has some identifiable political power. If the precinct is only a subdivision of a ward or other district, its leadership is usually appointed by the ward or district leader. But where the precinct itself is the basic unit with locally elected leadership, then it is like a ward or district. All such basic units will be referred to as precincts.

Precinct leadership is usually selected by local party members either in a formal election using ballots or voting machines, or in an informal election known as a "caucus." This caucus is simply a party meeting, where the members select their local leadership, usually by voice vote. The leader may be known as a chairman, committeeman, or captain. Often a co-leader or assistant leader is also chosen. In many areas a woman is usually second in command.

County and City Committees.   The governing political body in the party above the precinct level is a county or city committee. Often these committees are composed of the precinct leaders in the area. The committee selects a county or city chairman for the party, often, one of its members.

State Committees.   Still higher, at the state level, the key political unit in each major party is known as the state committee, state executive committee, or state central committee. Its membership may be selected in one of several ways. In some states it is composed of all the county and city chairmen, with perhaps their vice-chairmen also included. There may be direct election by party members, who select a state committee member from each state senate district, or several from each Congressional District to represent their district on the state committee. In some states, the party members select delegates to attend a county convention, or sometimes a state convention, at which the delegates from each area select a state committee member. Frequently a committee-man and committeewoman are chosen from each area of the state entitled to membership on the committee. The role of party members in choosing the state committee is thus either direct, or once removed, as in those cases where party members have chosen precinct leaders or convention delegates who in turn choose the members of the state committee.

The state committee chooses its own officers. The chairman is the most important. He need not necessarily be a member of the state committee. Sometimes, he is the personal choice of the party's most important elected officeholder in the state, usually the Governor, or occasionally a U. S. Senator, or the mayor of a large city. In other states, he is the free choice of the state committee members.

National Committees.   At the national level, both major parties have a national committee composed of at least two members from each state. A national committeeman and a national committee-woman are selected by each state's delegation to the Republican and Democratic national conventions. The Republican National Committee also includes the state chairmen from those states that recently elected a Republican Governor or U. S. Senator, or gave their electoral votes to the G.O.P.'s candidate for President.

Each national committee selects its chairman and other officers. The national chairman of the President's party is the personal choice of the President. The chairman of the opposition party is the personal choice of the party's presidential nominee. After an election in which the nominee has not been successful, however, his choice as chairman often resigns and is replaced by a new chairman agreeable to the party's key national leaders. Thus, after Barry Goldwater was defeated in 1964, Republican leaders insisted that his personal choice for G.O.P. chairman, Dean Burch, resign. To place the national chairmanship in the hands of someone less identified with any one leader or any one segment of the party's thinking, the Republican leaders selected Ray Bliss, then Republican State Chairman of Ohio.

Pyramid of Power. The formal structure of party government is thus seen to be, generally, in the form of a pyramid, with thousands of precinct leaders at the base, a tier of state leaders near the top, and national leadership at the peak. Frequently, one person holds several positions within the structure. The power he exercises depends on the highest position he holds, but his ability to retain power often depends on his lowest position.

For example, in the 1950's Carmine DeSapio was among the most powerful leaders in the Democratic Party in New York. From his positions as New York County leader and National Committeeman, he had an important voice in state and national party affairs. He was in a position to hold county leadership because he had been elected by party members to be leader of his local assembly district. When a rival group sought to challenge his power in the party, they fought him at the local level. In 1961 his opponents defeated him in a party primary for local party office—leader of his assembly district. Only a few thousand votes were cast, and DeSapio lost by 1,420 votes. Since, under New York party rules, only district leaders were eligible for election as county leader, that local defeat led to the loss of his state and national committee positions, and his fall from power in the Democratic Party.

The voice of rank and file party members does not often have such a dramatic impact upon party leadership at high levels. Yet the opportunity is there. In most states, party elections are held every two years. Local leaders and, sometimes, county or state officials must run for their party offices in party primaries. Only rarely are incumbents voted out, but examples such as the defeat of DeSapio remind all party leaders what can happen.

PARTY LEADERSHIP

Like any system of government, the government of politics is no better than the people who run it. In the first instance this means the party members who participate in the conduct of party affairs. Yet of the millions of members in each of the major political parties, only a very small percentage use their right of membership to vote for party officials.

Why do so few participate? Party elections often are not held on the same day as public elections, and many people will not take the trouble to vote more than once in the same year. In addition, people do not readily see any connection between a vote for party officials and its effect on public issues. Voters can get interested enough to participate when they realize that their vote can help decide which man becomes a Congressman or President. But, understandably, they do not have the same interest in voting for a man who will play only a minor role in party affairs. Often the only party leader elected directly by party members is the precinct leader. In some states a member of the state committee is directly elected. But the county chairman and the state chairman are always selected by the respective county- and state-level committees. As to these key officials, the party members do not have a direct vote; hence their lack of interest in party elections.

Local Party Leaders. The precinct leader's job is to know the voters of his precinct and to maintain such friendly year-round relationships with them that they will, more likely than not, follow his suggestion on election day. He probably has little influence on their vote for President, but where the candidates are less well known, as in an election for some local office or a party primary, the precinct leader's suggestion may carry considerable weight.

These local political leaders win their support by directing a personal appeal to the very small number of voters who make up a majority of those who bother to vote in party elections. A precinct leader often knows personally every party member who voted for him. For many he has done some personal favor.

Until the 1930's, the power of precinct leaders was built largely on the goodwill earned for past favors. When a family was hungry and cold, the neighborhood party chieftain brought food and a bucket of coal. When there was no job to be found, he arranged for one with the city public works department. When someone was in trouble with the law, he put in the "good word" that often brought favorable results from a prosecutor or a judge.

Today many of the services the precinct leader once rendered have been assumed by local and state welfare agencies. The needy family of today more often gets help from a social worker than from a precinct leader. Civil service reform has greatly reduced the number of available jobs on public payrolls to which some faithful party member can be appointed without regard to merit. And higher standards in government have lessened the opportunities for preferential treatment from public agencies and courts.

State and County Party Leaders. City, county, and state party leaders are usually the key figures in the government of politics. They hold positions of power. Normally they have reached their positions of leadership because they enjoy the confidence and support of many local leaders. This support is demonstrated in county and state nominating conventions when delegates, who have often been selected by precinct leaders, cast their votes for candidates supported by city, county, and state leaders.

Because they can exert influence on nominations, these party leaders are given a major voice by the public officeholders when the time comes to appoint deserving party members to various public positions. A Governor who secured his nomination through the help of several strong county leaders will often pay attention to their recommendations in filling positions in his administration. Then, once it becomes clear that these party leaders have a say in appointments to public positions, their power to command support from local political leaders increases. A precinct leader interested in recommending appointments after an election will exert all his influence to win nominations for the candidates favored by his county leader, especially if he believes the county leader will help make the decision on whether his recommendations are followed.

The man formally designated state chairman is not necessarily the most powerful state leader. He may be a compromise selection, agreeable to the leaders of two or more rival factions within a party. Or he may preside over a weak state committee which exerts no real influence over city and county leaders. In some states, however, the state chairman is the key man.

Who is the most powerful political leader in a state? He may be a leader of the formal political structure, a key public officeholder, or, occasionally, a person occupying no official position. The acknowledged Democratic political leader in Connecticut is John Bailey, the state chairman; in Illinois, Richard Daley, Mayor of Chicago; in Virginia, for many years it was the late U.S. Senator Harry Byrd. On the Republican side, the political leader of Rhode Island is Governor John Chafee; in Illinois, U. S. Senator Everett Dirksen; and in Ohio, for several years until he became G.O.P. National Chairman in 1965, the former state chairman, Ray Bliss. In some states, important political power is held by Congressmen, mayors, or national committeemen. In earlier years, there were several powerful state political leaders without any public or formal political position, whose power was based largely on their wealth. That behind-the-scenes political power is rarely found today.

> *In the 1850's the word "machine" acquired its political con-notation. The horse-drawn fire engines used in those days were called machines, and "running with the machine" meant chasing a fire engine. In New York City, the local political leader, William M. Tweed, owned a fire company whose employees were active in city politics. "Running with the machine" in New York City came to mean following the political dictates of "Boss" Tweed. In 1876, the political cartoonist Thomas Nast pictured the Democratic political organization in the city as a firefighting machine. Since then the label has been applied to any effective political organiza-tion with strong leadership. When criticized it's a machine; when praised it's an organization.*

The modern state political leader bears little resemblance to the "boss" of an earlier era. Today's party leader may exert consider-able influence on the political and governmental affairs of his state, but his methods and objectives differ from those of the old-style bosses. With rare exception, he has a far higher standard of honesty. He knows that corruption is bad politics, and he neither participates in it nor tolerates it in his organization. His objectives are far broader than simply maintaining the strength of his organization. He knows the public demands able candidates and enlightened stands on the issues. He works to see that his party supplies both. He can be tough and hard-headed. But he no longer wields power just for its own sake. He recognizes a public interest in politics, and he aspires to lead a political organization that works effectively in the public interest.

Party leaders often look to the elder statesmen of the party for guidance. Among Republicans these include their last four presidential candidates Barry Goldwater, Dwight D. Eisenhower, Richard M. Nixon, and Thomas E. Dewey.

National Party Leaders. Political leaders at the national level are usually those state leaders whose strength within their own political organizations is strong enough to give them influence beyond their state borders. The state or county chairman with enough influence to command the allegiance of a number of delegates to a national nominating convention is by that fact alone a national party leader. He may have more power than the members of the national committee from his state. In some states these national committee members may be political powers in their own right; in other states, they are subservient appointees of state leaders.

National Chairman of the Party. The role and power of the party's national chairman depends, first, on whether his party controls the White House and, secondly, on the combination of forces that led to his selection. The chairman of the President's party plays whatever role the President wants him to play. The chairman may be a key figure in advising the President on Federal patronage positions, as James Farley was under Franklin D. Roosevelt, or he may at best share this power with the President's personal advisors at the White House and elsewhere. The extent to which he becomes a party spokesman on public issues is also in the President's discretion.

The chairman of the national party out of power is rarely concerned with patronage. His task is to keep the party strong enough to make a successful national campaign in the next election. Without the power and the public forum of the White House to help him, he faces a difficult task. If he is the handpicked choice of the defeated candidate, the followers of rival candidates will be suspicious of him. If the defeated candidate's chairman steps aside, the replacement is likely to be a compromise candidate to whom the various factions will extend cooperation but not real power.

The national chairmen of both parties spend much of their time visiting state leaders across the country, discussing political problems of mutual concern, bringing a rousing message to local political dinners, and generally working to maintain a national party spirit. Always their eyes are fixed on the midterm election two years away and beyond that to the next presidential election.

PARTY ORGANIZATION IN ACTION

The activities of party organizations vary tremendously from one area to another. In one state the party may be strong and effective, with daily activity. In another state, the party may be no more than a paper organization, rousing itself at rare intervals only to comply with state requirements for the selection of party candidates.

Personnel and tradition seem to account for many of the differences among party organizations. A state party that has been lazy in the past can become an aggressive organization when new, energetic leaders come to power.

Before 1956, for example, Republican Party activity in the South was so listless that the party rarely bothered even to nominate candidates for most public offices. Democratic victories were conceded. After 1956, however, a new crop of young political leaders breathed life into the G.O.P. in several Southern states. As a result of their efforts, the party now contests elections for offices from city council to U. S. Senator. Their successes since 1960 include Republican wins by a Senator from Texas, governors in Arkansas and Florida, Congressmen from several states and many state legislators and city officials.

The hold of tradition is also important. Politics is essentially a conservative activity: what has been done before determines what is most likely to be done again. The old ways do change, but slowly and often not until those in power have been replaced through age or political upheaval. A tradition of strong party activity perpetuates acceptance of party strength, while a history of weak organizations makes people suspicious of efforts to exert strong political power.

Keeping Control. The first task of all party organizations is to maintain control of positions of party leadership. In any state that is well organized politically, the leaders of each party at all levels are in an alliance to maintain themselves in power. Rival factions may vie for power in one city or one county, but the state party leadership will often stand back from these local controversies and quickly acknowledge the leadership of the local winning faction. The new city or county leader will soon find a place in the alliance of state leaders of his party. Within each city or county, the local party leadership works hard to prevent a rival faction from gaining enough strength to mount a serious challenge. Political organizations dislike outright confrontations within their ranks, because they know their party will be weakened and the opposition party will benefit.

Local revolutions do occur, however, and these intra-party fights are the most bitter in politics. The hostility that develops when a precinct leadership is fought for in a primary, or when several precincts are contested with county leadership at stake, is far more intense than in any election contest between candidates of opposite parties.

Some changes in party leadership occur without all-out contests between rival factions. At the state level, new candidates for Governor often demand the selection of new state party chairmen. Between 1960 and 1964, the position of Republican state chairman changed hands in two-thirds of the states.

Party Headquarters. The party organization usually maintains a state headquarters, and similar offices are in operation in large cities and counties. Depending on the condition of party finances, offices may be a one-room store front or a suite of hotel rooms. Standard equipment includes at least a mimeograph machine, lists of registered voters, and vast quantities of campaign literature. A full-time executive director is often in charge of headquarters. He keeps in touch with party officials throughout the area, acts as liaison between elected officeholders and the party organization, and generally provides continuity to party affairs.

Also at party headquarters on most days is a loyal band of party workers. Holding no special positions, they show up faithfully to do the chores, swap political gossip, and offer opinions to anyone willing to listen. Their reward is sometimes a minor job on a public payroll, more often just the fun and excitement of mixing with the mighty and feeling useful at the nerve center of political activity.

Political Clubs. To maintain interest among party members, some organizations, especially in the cities, establish political clubs on a neighborhood basis. Some 20,000 are in existence, many organized on nationality lines. For most members the clubs are mainly social, a place to meet new friends who live nearby. The party organizations find them a useful way of keeping members interested in party activities. An occasional speech by one of the party's public officeholders reminds the club members of the party's objectives. The organization also runs picnics and dances to keep the faithful happy and to provide some fun and enjoyment in return for the hard work that will be asked for as election day draws near.

Patronage. The party organization works continually with public officeholders on patronage. In its broadest sense, patronage includes any benefit those in public office can bestow on others. Jobs are especially important. They range from the major appointments to such government positions as judges and heads of key agencies, to the minor jobs in a county public works department or a state highway department. In addition, officeholders can reward many public-spirited citizens by appointment as members of advisory committees or trustees of public institutions. These positions carry no pay but often much prestige.

The organization of the party whose officeholder has the power to make the appointment usually recommends one or more people for the position to be filled. Sometimes the organization's choice automatically gets the job. At other times, the officeholder submits his choice to the party for political "clearance"—making sure that the person slated for the appointment is acceptable to party leaders from his precinct, city, county, and state.

Sometimes the person who gets the job is not nearly so important as the political leader who backed him for the job. Except for direct clashes in primaries for party offices, rival political leaders have few chances to demonstrate their strength. Backing rival candidates for an important appointive job presents a clear opportunity to show party members which political leader is in favor with key officeholders. The leader who successfully recommends a candidate for appointment by a mayor, a Governor, or the President, demonstrates his influence in city, state, or national politics.

The number of appointive positions varies widely from one state to another. The Governor of Pennsylvania is said to be able to fill 50,000 state jobs; the Governor of New Jersey, 18,000. In other states, the total may be barely 100 full-time jobs in executive departments and another 100 on part-time boards and commissions.

Besides appointive jobs, other benefits of patronage are the award of business contracts and the minor preferential treatment obtained from all levels of government. City, state, and national governments always require business services from insurance agents, building contractors, appraisers, lawyers, accountants, and others. Not all of these services are put up for public competitive bidding. The party in power often has opportunities to award contracts for such services to people and firms that have supported the party. So long as the work needs to be done for a legitimate public purpose and the fees charged are reasonable, there is no impropriety. But there always exists the danger that a contract will be awarded at a higher price to a political supporter than at the lower price which competitive bidding would have produced. Inevitably some abuses do occur.

Favoritism from public officeholders is the most questionable form of patronage. Some local party leaders, anxious to show their followers how influential they are, prevail upon those in public office to extend favors. At the least, this may mean "fixing" a traffic ticket. At the worst, a state or federal agency may rule in favor of an applicant who can generate political pressure. At issue may be an award of public funds or a valuable franchise. The agency is supposed to decide these questions on their merits and in the public interest, but politics sometimes weights the scales. Abuses in these fields usually lead to trouble and become political issues in campaigns. Wise officeholders keep such abuses in check.

Towards the Campaign. As election season approaches, the party organizations gear up for intense activity. The mechanics of the nominating process are largely in their hands. The parties hold nominating conventions, primaries, or a combination of both, depending on prevailing state law. Once the parties' nominees are selected, the campaign battles for votes begin. The major parties confront each other in contests for most offices throughout the land. A loose coalition of 50 state Republican Party organizations stands opposed to a similar collection of 50 state Democratic organizations. From national chairman to precinct captain the ranks are filled by hard-working, dedicated men and women. Proud to be called politicians, they do the political work that makes a democratic system of government succeed.

6

THE
NOMINATING
PROCESS

Winning public office requires success in two contests—the battle for a nomination and the campaign for election. Whether the office is city alderman or President, the ultimate winner must first win his party's nomination before challenging the opposing party's candidate. The nominating process narrows the field from the many who hope for public office down to the two major party candidates who will square off in the general election.

Sometimes the nominating process is even more important than the election itself. This happens in those areas of the country where one of the parties is so strong that its candidate always wins the election. The Democratic candidate for Congress from Brooklyn, for example, or the Republican nominee from rural Kansas is sure to beat his opponent. In some Southern districts, the Democratic candidate does not even have a Republican opponent. In fact, in nearly three-fourths of all Congressional Districts, the candidate of the dominant party usually receives at least 55% of the vote, a big enough margin to almost guarantee his next election on the day he is nominated.

Naturally, the more surely a nomination leads to election, the more competition there is among the hopefuls to become the party's candidate. The nomination fight for a "safe" seat is as hard fought as any election. When House Speaker Sam Rayburn died in 1961, after representing the 4th District of Texas for 48 years, the primary election to select the Democratic candidate for this district drew 6 contenders. On the other hand, where election prospects are hopeless, the minority party often has to persuade someone to accept a nomination.

An ambitious person, however, will often become a candidate in a district where his party fares badly. First, he gains public attention even in losing, especially if he runs better than previous nominees of his party. He may then be rewarded with an appointed position or nomination for some other office where he has a better chance. Secondly, no matter how regularly his party has lost, there is always the hope that this election will be different—and sometimes it is. In 1959, Edmund S. Muskie became the first Democratic Senator from Maine in 42 years; in 1961, John Tower became the first Republican Senator from Texas in 84 years.

Political parties use two basic methods for nominating their candidates: the convention and the primary. A *convention* is a meeting of selected party members chosen to represent local units of the party. A *primary* is an election open to all party members, and, in some states, open to all voters. Sometimes, the nominating process is a combination of both methods. For example, in Colorado, Massachusetts, and Nebraska, conventions endorse the party's choice but the voters then decide in a primary whether the party's choice or someone else will be the nominee.

The convention is a form of representative government; the primary at its best is pure democracy.

CONVENTIONS

Conventions are held to nominate candidates for offices at all levels of government, from the community to the nation at large. A city convention will name candidates for mayor (if this office is elected on a partisan basis), and for state representatives and state senators to serve in the state legislature. A district or county convention will name candidates for U. S. Representative and such other regional positions as county commissioner and sheriff. A state convention will name candidates for statewide offices such as Governor, U. S. Senator, lieutenant governor, and attorney general. The great national conventions select candidates for the national offices of President and Vice President of the United States.

Apart from the national conventions, the use of the convention to nominate candidates has declined sharply since 1900. Only

Connecticut and Rhode Island use this process extensively, though a few others, including New York and Michigan, use it to select candidates for statewide offices. Many states that now select candidates in primaries still have party conventions, usually every two years, to adopt a party platform.

Most of the delegates to local and state conventions are dedicated party workers — the men and women who work year round, and especially at election time, to help the party win. Attendance at the convention recognizes their place in the party hierarchy. Normally, the delegates will follow the advice of the party leaders from their community in deciding whom to support. But this is a two-way street. The wise leader makes his "recommendation" only after individual conversations with his city or county delegation to measure their own sentiments.

Generally, the major disputes at a state convention are not within local delegations, but rather between delegations from different parts of the state. Major cities or sections of the state often support a candidate from their own area. Once a decision is made to support one area's choice for the nomination for Governor, the candidates for the other offices on the state ticket are usually selected from other areas so that all sections of the state will be represented. Sometimes, party leaders also try to "balance" the ticket by selecting candidates of different religious and ethnic backgrounds.

Party Control of Conventions. Where still in use, the convention device tends to keep the nominating process under the control of the party leadership. Consider, for example, a state convention called to nominate a candidate for Governor. The delegates have been selected either by delegates to local conventions or by members of local party committees, either of which have, in turn, been chosen by the local party membership. In either case, the state convention delegates are two steps removed from the rank and file party members. The local leader generally has a major, if not decisive, say as to who serves on the local committee or who attends the local convention. In this way the local party leadership has control in the selection of delegates to the state convention. The decisions that the delegates finally make at the state convention are thus largely in the hands of the party leaders who arranged for their attendance.

This fact of party-leadership control does not necessarily produce bad results, especially in states where there is close competition between the two major parties in the general election. The party leadership knows that to win the election it must arrange for the nomination of candidates with broad appeal to the voters. So when the party leaders urge their choice of candidate upon the convention delegates, they cannot afford to back cronies whom the public would reject. Instead the leaders must use their best judgment in recommending candidates the voters will support.

If they guess wrong too often, they will soon be deposed as party leaders. Only if they predict public sentiment and back winning candidates will they succeed.

While the convention system tends to keep power within the party leadership, new party members can make their influence felt. For the party membership in each precinct forms the base of the convention structure, as of the party structure itself. As new people become active in the party, they can challenge the leadership of their precinct, and if successful, they are then in a position to influence the selection of delegates. From this foothold, they can join forces with like-minded insurgents in other parts of the state. The coalition they forge can challenge and ultimately replace the party leadership and gain the decisive voice in the nomination of candidates.

Such a major upheaval does not happen often, but it can be done. Just the possibility of such an uprising keeps smart party leaders attentive to the views of newcomers in the ranks.

THE PRIMARY

Shortly after 1900, dissatisfaction with the convention system for nominating candidates led to the adoption of the direct primary. Wisconsin was the first state to make the primary mandatory for the nomination of statewide candidates. The forces of reform soon prevailed in one state after another to adopt the system that was supposed to take the nominating power away from the political leaders and place it directly in the hands of the voters. Some form of a primary is now in use in almost every state.

In essence, a primary is a preliminary election in which the voters of each party select the men and women who will be their party's candidates in the general election. Often, more than two contenders for a nomination run in a primary, and the person with the most votes wins, even if he fails to get a majority of all the votes cast. In some Southern states a majority of the votes is required for nomination. If no contender wins at least half the votes, then the two with the highest number of votes enter a second contest, called a run-off primary, to decide the winner.

Normally, primary elections are held in the spring or early fall of election years. In most states, prospective candidates can secure a place on the primary ballot simply by announcing their candidacy for a nomination and securing a few hundred signatures (several thousand in some states) on a nominating petition. State law specifies how many signatures and who is eligible to sign a nominating petition. Generally, any registered voter is eligible.

The rules determining who can vote in a primary vary considerably among the states. Most states use the "closed" primary: only members of a political party may vote to select that party's candidates. Party membership is determined either from the permanent list of registered voters or from some inquiry at the time the voter comes to vote in the primary. In these "closed" primaries, independent voters with no formal party affiliation are excluded from voting for party candidates. A few states hold "open" primary contests: all voters, regardless of their party affiliation, are eligible to vote in the primary of either party. This type of primary permits members of one party to "cross over" and vote in the other party's primary. By doing so they can help to nominate as the opposition candidate the man they believe is the easiest to defeat. Then, in the general election, these "cross over" voters support the choice of their own party, whom they favored all along.

In many respects the primary campaign and election are conducted just like the final campaign and election between the nominated candidates. Those seeking nomination make speeches, appear on radio and television, advertise in newspapers and on billboards, and go through all the steps of an election campaign. On primary day the contenders do whatever they can to assure a large turnout of their supporters at the polls. Votes are cast at the same polling places and by the same method — paper ballot or voting machine — as in the general election.

Primaries vs. General Elections. The differences between the primary and the final election are significant. First, the candidates for the nomination must bear in mind that, after the primary, the losing contenders will be expected to support the winning nominee in the big battle against the opposing party's nominee. This means there ought to be some caution in the type of criticism and attack the contenders in the primary direct at each other. Many primary compaigns proceed this way, with the contenders emphasizing their own strengths, rather than their opponents weaknesses.

In some contests, however, as the campaign progresses, tempers rise, the desire to win overwhelms, and before long the contenders are battling each other as hard as they would the opposition party. The aftermath of such a bruising contest can seriously handicap the primary winner. Those who supported his opponents do not soon forget the sharpness of his attack on their favorites. The scars inflicted in a primary campaign often do not heal until long after the general election.

A second major difference is the low proportion of voters who bother to vote in a primary. In most primary elections the turnout of eligible voters is less than 35%, and sometimes the figure drops to 10% or even 5%. Most voters take the trouble to go to the polls only on the day of the final election. Those who vote in primaries are the ones who take a great interest in local party affairs.

These facts lead to a third difference — the increased role of the party leadership in determining the outcome. At the start, the party leaders play a major role in determining whether there will be a contested primary at all. Knowing the potential damage to the party that can result from a bitter fight, the leaders do their best to seek agreement on a candidate within the party ranks. Often they persuade contending hopefuls to step out of the race by the lure of some lesser present reward — perhaps an appointive position — or some greater future reward — the nomination next time. This effort often succeeds, and many primaries are really little more than a ratification at the polls of the choice made by the party leaders.

Even where contenders insist on running, the party leadership is often able to control the outcome by supporting one of the hopefuls. In some states, the decision to support one of the contenders is formalized by a vote of the party's local or state committee or by a pre-primary convention. In other states, the party's endorsement is informally made by the party leadership but unmistakably communicated to the party workers. Some party organizations remain scrupulously neutral in primary campaigns, except to endorse incumbents seeking renomination.

Regardless of method, the fact of party support is generally sufficient to insure the nomination of the party's choice. The outcome is in the hands of the very few who bother to vote, and these are the people most ready to follow the recommendation of the party leadership. Occasionally, a strong and popular personality emerges who can successfully overcome the party's endorsed candidate and win the party's nomination for himself.

Minor Party Candidacies.   There are two other ways in which voters have an opportunity to place candidates in contention for a general election. A person not nominated by either of the major parties can petition to appear on the November ballot as the candidate of some third party or as an Independent candidate. State laws vary on this subject, but normally this petition requires the signatures of a fixed percentage of the voters in the last election, sometimes 1%. This may amount to a requirement of several thousand signatures, usually too great a burden for most minor candidates to bear. Of course, minor parties that have regularly won a minimum number of votes in past elections are entitled to have their parties' nominees placed on the ballot. In some states four or five minor parties regularly nominate a slate of candidates, sometimes endorsing some of the same candidates nominated by one of the major parties.

Most state election laws also permit voters to write in the name of their choice, even if the name has not been printed on the ballot. This method usually produces no more than a handful of votes. But as with most things in politics, there are exceptions to every rule. In 1954, J. Strom Thurmond, running in a Democratic primary, won a write-in vote of 143,444 and became his party's nominee and ultimately U. S. Senator from South Carolina. In 1964, Henry Cabot Lodge won the New Hampshire presidential primary with a write-in vote of 33,007.

NOMINATING PRESIDENTIAL CANDIDATES

Selection of candidates for the Presidency is a special event in American politics. Both major parties use a complicated system, involving state conventions and primaries which select delegates to attend the great national conventions. These conventions not only select party candidates for President and Vice President, but also serve as the one national assembly of the political leaders from the 50 state party organizations.

Development of National Conventions. When our nation was founded, we had no national conventions. The men who wrote the Constitution made no provision for conventions because they did not foresee the development of a two-party political system. They thought that the members of the electoral college would exercise their own judgment and select a President from among the outstanding figures of the country. That was the way George Washington was chosen.

As soon as national parties formed, however, they had to find some method to select presidential candidates. At first this job was done by each party's membership in Congress. Senators and Representatives of the two early parties, the Federalists and the Democratic-Republicans, met in a caucus of their own members to select candidates for President and Vice-President. As the parties grew, the caucus system soon became unpopular because participation was limited to members of Congress.

In 1831, a minor party, the Anti-Mason Party, held the first national convention to choose candidates for President and Vice-President. Later that year, the National Republicans held a national convention in Baltimore and nominated Henry Clay as their presidential candidate. In May, 1832, the Democratic Party held its first national convention, endorsed Andrew Jackson for a second term, and named Martin Van Buren as his running mate. By 1844, the national convention had become established.

The Convention's Unifying Effect. The national convention is the one great unifying force that holds together the 50 state organizations of the major political parties. The presidential nominating event every four years is really the only occasion when these separate state parties must come together and function, if only for a week, as a national organization. Only if they cooperate can they win the greatest political prize—the Presidency.

The requirement of at least majority agreement upon a candidate who must seek support from all the voters of the country serves to maintain the national aspect of our two political parties. And the majority agreement should be acceptable to the minority of the convention. In 1912, the Republican convention's nomination of William Howard Taft was so unacceptable to a minority of the delegates that later, in a separate convention, they nominated Teddy Roosevelt to run as a third party (Progressive) candidate. This split in Republican forces resulted in defeat for both men and the election of the Democrat, Woodrow Wilson. The lesson of 1912 showed both parties the importance of selecting a candidate acceptable throughout the party.

Occasionally a party can risk revolt by one group of supporters without suffering defeat. In 1948, the Democratic national convention renominated President Harry Truman. A group of Southern delegates were so opposed to Truman's liberal position on civil rights and other issues that they walked out of the convention, held a convention of their own, and nominated J. Strom Thurmond as their "States' Rights" candidate. Thurmond polled more than 1 million votes and won the 39 electoral votes of four states, but even this loss of Democratic support failed to prevent Truman's victory. On the other hand, in 1964, a sizable number of Republicans were dissatisfied with the Republican national convention's choice of Barry Goldwater. Rather than nominate a candidate of their own, they simply cast their votes for Lyndon Johnson, increasing his election victory to a landslide margin.

Selecting the Delegates.   The convention originates in the states with the selection of delegates who will vote to nominate their party's candidate. The rules of each national party determine how many votes are allotted to each state. In earlier years, each state was entitled to as many votes in a national convention as it had in the electoral college—the number of its U. S. Senators (2) plus its U. S. Representatives (1 to 43, depending on the state's population). Later the allotment was doubled to permit more delegates to participate. This plan gave each state nominating strength roughly proportionate to its population.

In the 20th century both parties became dissatisfied with this system because it failed to recognize the strength of each state party. Republican party organizations in the South, for example, were once virtually nonexistent between conventions and contributed no electoral votes to the party's candidate, yet they had as many votes at the convention as other states of equal size.

The Republicans, in 1916, and the Democrats, in 1940, again changed their rules to give extra convention votes according to the way each state voted in the previous election. For example, in 1964, Kansas and Mississippi each had a population of just over 2 million. At the Republican national convention Mississippi had 13 votes, but Kansas, because of its support of Nixon in 1960 and the election of Republican congressional candidates in 1962, was allotted 20 votes. In this way the states that vote Republican have an added say as to who will be the Republican candidate, and Democratic states have a larger voice in choosing the Democratic candidate.[1]

Party rules, generally, leave the method of selecting delegates up to each state. In most states, the delegates are picked by state conventions or by the state committees of each political party. As with the designation of statewide candidates for public office, these methods keep power largely in the hands of the party leadership. At those times when the party leaders are publicly committed to a particular candidate for the party's presidential nomination, they, generally, have the power to arrange for the selection of delegates who will vote for their choice. At other times, party leaders find it preferable to withhold any public commitment and come to the con-

---

[1] By 1964 both parties had made their systems for allotting convention delegates fairly complicated. In the Democratic convention, each state was entitled to 3 votes for each electoral vote, plus 10 votes if the state gave its electoral votes to Kennedy in 1960, plus 1 vote for every 100,000 popular votes cast for Kennedy in 1960, and in no event less than its 1960 convention total.

In the Republican convention, each state was entitled to 4 votes — 2 for each U. S. Senator, plus 2 votes for each U. S. Representative-at-Large, plus 6 votes if the state gave its electoral votes to Nixon in 1960 or elected a Republican Governor or Senator in 1960 or 1962, plus 1 vote for each Congressional District that cast at least 2,000 popular votes for Nixon in 1960 or for the Republican congressional candidate in 1962, plus 1 vote for each Congressional District that cast at least 10,000 popular votes for Nixon in 1960 or for the Republican congressional candidate in 1962.

vention with delegates whose decisions will not be made until the very last moment.

In 19 states, the law provides for some form of presidential primary election in which voters can determine either who will be the delegates to the national conventions or which candidate the delegates will vote for. The voters elect convention delegates in California, Florida, Massachusetts, New Hampshire, New Jersey, Ohio, Oregon, Pennsylvania, South Dakota, West Virginia, and Wisconsin. Of these 11 states, Ohio requires those running for convention delegate to indicate their preference for presidential candidate, and almost all the other states in the group permit an indication of preference. In these states, voters sometimes have a real choice between rival slates of delegates, each pledged to support different contenders for the presidential nomination. In Illinois, Nebraska, and New York, part of the state delegation to the national convention is elected in the primary, and part is chosen at the state's convention. State law permits, but does not require, election of delegates in Alabama, Arkansas, and Rhode Island.

In nine states—Illinois, Indiana, Maryland, Nebraska, New Hampshire, New Jersey, Oregon, Pennsylvania, and West Virginia —the primary ballot contains the names of the presidential contenders themselves. However, the voters' preference, as expressed in these nine primaries, is binding upon the convention delegates only in Indiana, Maryland, and Oregon.[2]

Voting in presidential delegate or preference primaries is open only to party members, except in Wisconsin where any voter may vote for delegates to either party's convention.

A direct clash between the leading contenders for each party's nomination, usually, occurs in no more than four or five presidential primary states, and sometimes only in two or three. Contenders pick the primaries they will enter with care, challenging an opponent face to face only when they feel they will win or when it would be too embarrassing not to try. In almost every presidential primary state, a candidate's name appears on the ballot only with his consent.

There is no certainty, however, that the primary results will

---

[2] In Maryland and Indiana, the delegates, bound by the preference primary, are selected by state or local conventions.

affect the ultimate choice of the national conventions. Often they prove only who will *not* be nominated. Wendell Willkie's 1944 loss in the Wisconsin Republican primary and Estes Kefauver's 1956 loss in the California Democratic primary ended their prospects in those years. Yet primary winners are by no means assured of nomination. Teddy Roosevelt captured most of the Republican primaries in 1912, but lost the nomination. The same fate befell Estes Kefauver in 1952, after winning most of the Democratic primaries.

Sometimes, however, the presidential primary does have a major bearing on the eventual winner. In 1960, John F. Kennedy could not have been nominated had he not won the primary contests against Hubert Humphrey in Wisconsin and West Virginia. These victories convinced state leaders throughout the country of his ability to win votes. The primaries can always break and, sometimes, make a presidential nominee.

The Convention Assembles. So it happens that on a usually hot day in midsummer of years divisible by 4, thousands of delegates and alternates converge on the convention city.[3] Since this large number of people will spend a considerable amount of money entertaining themselves in the holiday atmosphere of a convention, cities compete to be selected as the convention site. Several cities will offer to pay for a portion of the convention expenses. In 1964, San Francisco and Atlantic City each paid $650,000 to be selected. The host city must also have a large auditorium, many hotels, and sufficient recreational facilities.

The delegates include most of the Governors, and many Senators and Congressmen. As a group they are well educated—about 80% attended college. The great majority are lawyers, businessmen, and other professional people. About one-tenth are women.

For most of the delegates the trip is more like a vacation, with the

---

[3] In 1964, the Republican convention consisted of 1,308 delegates and 1,308 alternates. The Democratic convention had 2,944 delegates and 2,308 alternates.

The position of "alternate delegate" was created to give each party more opportunities to reward faithful party workers by including them in the delegation. An alternate rarely has anything official to do at a convention. Occasionally, a delegate permits his alternate to take his place on the convention floor.

The pandemonium and excitement that breaks out on the convention floor when a presidential candidate is nominated is one of the most colorful sights in American politics.

added thrill of participating in one of the most colorful events in our nation. It is a chance to meet and renew acquaintances with party people from other states. Very few of the delegates will have to wrestle with their consciences in deciding how to cast their vote. That decision will, generally, have been made by the state convention that sent them, or by the voters in the presidential primary that elected them, or by the delegation leaders whose judgment they are willing to follow. In some instances, especially where party organization is not strong, a state contingent will include delegates who are strictly "on their own." The choice of the presidential nominee is theirs to make, and the candidates woo these uncommitted delegates individually.

For the most part, however, the real decision-making power in the national convention is in the hands of the political leaders of the states, especially of those states with a large number of convention votes. Most of these leaders have made their decision before the convention begins, casting their lot, early, with a presidential hopeful so that he will be especially grateful to them if he should go on to be nominated and elected. A few choose to stay neutral until the balloting starts, figuring that greater gratitude will go to the leader who delivers not the first ballots but the last, decisive ones. Sometimes a state's delegation stays neutral between the leading contenders on the first ballot by giving its votes to a "favorite son" — a popular Governor or U. S. Senator from its own state, who is not a serious presidential candidate. Then on the second ballot, the delegation, free of its initial commitment, dramatically shifts its support to one of the principal contenders.

Balloting — The Crucial Day. The day of the presidential nomination is the key day at the national convention. First, each of the several candidates is formally placed in nomination by a well-known speaker, generally from his own state. This nominating speech is followed by the traditional demonstration, a colorful, noisy parade through the convention hall. Each candidate's supporters don zany hats, wave signs hailing their hero, cheer wildly, and, stampeded into action, march exuberantly around the hall with encouragement from brass bands.

No such demonstration has ever been known to add a single delegate to a candidate's total, but no major candidate has ever been known to forego the demonstration in his honor. After all the candidates have been placed in nomination and all the seconding speeches concluded — a process often lasting eight hours — the roll of states is called, and each delegation chairman announces the votes from his state.

There is no set pattern to convention balloting. It depends on the number of leading contenders and their individual strength. A two-man contest turns simply on who has the majority, as Eisenhower showed when he beat Taft in 1952. Even in a field of hopefuls, one candidate may, by careful and aggressive work before the convention, produce a first-ballot majority, as Kennedy did in 1960, and Goldwater did in 1964. An incumbent President seeking a second term can, nowadays, be certain of renomination, though this was not true in the 19th century.

Even when there is no contest for the top nomination of the party, a noisy demonstration on behalf of the party choice adds greatly to the pageantry of the assembly.

Where three or more candidates have some, but not decisive, strength, then the drama of the convention heightens as successive ballots are necessary before one candidate wins a majority. Before 1936, the Democratic nominee had to win two-thirds of the convention's votes. This requirement increased the possibility of deadlock. In 1924, when 102 ballots failed to give either leading contender a two-thirds vote, a dramatic convention then compromised on a third choice, John W. Davis.

Even the majority rule now used by both parties can lead to stalemate. Republicans, in 1920, went through nine ballots before party leaders abandoned the front-runners and agreed on a comparative "dark horse," Warren G. Harding, who was, at that time, U. S. Senator from the state of Ohio.

The ultimate choice of the convention is based on many things. First, there is the candidates' public record. After many years in public life, the leading contenders have usually acquired some national following. Their accomplishments and resulting popularity have placed them in the running. Next, comes the assessment by party leaders as to which one would make the best President and which one is most likely to be elected. Finally, there is a difficult decision for party leaders and uncommitted delegates: whom should they support after their own favorite fails to win? This second-choice decision is often crucial. Franklin D. Roosevelt was nominated in 1932, when the California and the Texas delegates switched their votes to him after supporting House Speaker John N. Garner, most likely on the assurance that Garner would be named as FDR's running mate.

A decision made in a "smoke-filled room" refers to a meeting of key party leaders who, before or during a convention, agree upon a candidate they will support. The meeting often lasts late into the night, and many of those attending enjoy a good cigar.

The term gained popularity at the 1920 Republican National Convention in Chicago. Harry Daugherty, campaign manager for Ohio Senator Warren G. Harding, publicly predicted how Harding would be selected:

"Well, there will be no nomination on the early ballots. After the other candidates have failed, after they have gone their limit, the leaders, worn out and wishing to do the very best thing, will get together in some hotel room about 2:11 in the morning. Some 15 men, bleary-eyed with lack of sleep, and perspiring profusely with the excessive heat, will sit down around a big table. I will be with them and will present the name of Senator Harding. When the time comes, Harding will be selected, because he fits in perfectly with every need of the party and nation. He is the logical choice, and the leaders will determine to throw their support to him."

Just as Daugherty predicted, Republican leaders met late one night during the deadlocked convention, in Room 404 of the Blackstone Hotel. Harding was discussed, agreed upon, later nominated, and elected President. Daugherty missed only one point: he was not in the smoke-filled room. Since he had predicted what would happen, party leaders thought it would be embarrassing to invite him.

While Lyndon B. Johnson was being nominated at the 1964 Democratic convention, Hubert H. Humphrey, the President's personal choice for the Vice Presidency, accompanied him on the flight to the convention.

Choosing the Vice-Presidential Candidate. The convention's presidential candidate normally chooses his own vice-presidential running mate. The delegates simply ratify his decision. However, this has not always been so. Teddy Roosevelt was certainly not McKinley's choice at the Republican convention of 1900. Republican delegates, in 1920, not only failed to consult Harding on his preference, but rejected their leaders' choice and selected Calvin Coolidge.

The presidential candidate's choice, even when followed, is not just his personal whim. He normally consults carefully with all factions within his party and then urges the convention to name a man with broad support, especially in those parts of the country where the presidential nominee himself is not strong.

There was a time when the second place on the ticket was filled with virtually no regard to the possibility of that man becoming President. Yet of our 35 Presidents, 8 were Vice Presidents who took office at the death of a President. The recent growth in the importance of the office of Vice President and the tragic reminder of the Kennedy assassination have upgraded the seriousness of the choice of running mate. Kennedy's choice of Lyndon Johnson and Johnson's choice of Hubert Humphrey were clearly based on their own decision, shared by many within their party, as to who was best qualified to become President.

In 1956, the Democratic presidential nominee, Adlai Stevenson, took an unusual course: he made no recommendation and left the choice of his running mate to the convention delegates. In that dramatic contest, Senator Kefauver won the spot, narrowly defeating a young Senator from Massachusetts, John F. Kennedy.

The Party Platform. The only other major task of the convention is the writing of the party's platform. This is a long policy statement, setting forth the party's criticism of the opposition party and its own pledges of action if successful in the coming election. Where an incumbent President seeks renomination, he is in complete control of the platform writing, for the document is a defense of his record and a future commitment of what he plans to do. When the party out of power writes a platform, its content is generally drawn from the views of the leading contenders for the presidential nomination.

If a candidate comes to the convention with great delegate strength, his supporters will normally have a majority on the committee that writes the platform, and his views will therefore prevail. That was certainly the case when supporters of Senator Goldwater wrote the Republican platform in 1964.

The platforms of the two major parties are different in their fundamental outlook. Reciting these differences every four years is a useful exercise; it requires the parties to express their philosophies in terms of the current issues facing the country. Usually the platform omits specific statements of what the party intends, relying instead on general announcements of policy. And it often happens that a party once in power fails to carry through on some of the pledges contained in its platform. This has led many voters to ignore the platforms altogether. Yet despite vagueness and lack of binding commitment, the platform does maintain a philosophical identity for the party.

Sometimes, the platform forces a party to face up to an issue that divides its own supporters. This happened dramatically, in 1948, when the Democratic convention erupted into a floor fight over a plank on civil rights. Proponents of a strong stand on civil rights won, causing many Southern delegates to walk out of the

Fred Ward from Black Star

In order to be successful, a candidate should get an early start in his campaign. The late arrival of Governor William Scranton of Pennsylvania in the presidential race of 1964 was one reason why he was unable to win his party's support.

convention and, temporarily, out of the party to support a "States Rights" candidate of their own, J. Strom Thurmond. This battle had a lasting impact on the Democratic Party. Since 1948 the Democratic Party has taken an increasingly stronger stand on the vital issue of civil rights.

Seeking the Presidential Nomination.   From the standpoint of the contenders, the presidential nominating process is the supreme political obstacle course — exhausting, unpredictable, treacherous, and expensive.

In modern political history the nomination victories of John F. Kennedy, in 1960, and Barry Goldwater, in 1964, are possibly the best examples of a successfully planned campaign to become a presidential candidate. Both began their quest for the nomination three years before the national conventions. Their activity focused on two objectives: gaining a favorable national reputation among voters, and winning assurances of support from convention delegates. To impress the public at large, both men traveled the country extensively, accepting speaking engagements by the hundreds. They wrote books and articles. Leading magazines printed feature stories about them, their careers, their families, and their viewpoints.

The pursuit of delegates began long before the delegates were selected. Goldwater supporters went to work in several states during 1962 and 1963 to win control of the Republican county committees and county conventions that would select national convention delegates in 1964. Kennedy's political scouts made frequent visits to Democratic party leaders in many states two years before the 1960 national convention. Assurance of substantial delegate strength was won in New England and New York before a single delegate was chosen. Both men entered presidential primaries, with Kennedy scoring crucial wins in Wisconsin and West Virginia, and Goldwater clinching his bid with a narrow victory in California.

Goldwater arrived at the 1964 Republican convention with a clear majority of the delegates already legally bound or else publicly committed to support him. In 1960, Kennedy reached the Democratic convention with very close to a majority of delegates, and in the few days before the balloting began, he won assurances of enough support to make his nomination certain. The preparations of both men and their personal organizations were so thorough and so successful that the rollcall of delegates was only a formality that confirmed their hard-fought victories.

Whether or not substantial delegate support has been assured before the convention, contenders still solicit support from each delegate from the day the delegate is named in his home state until the convention balloting begins. One of the first major candidates to contact delegates on an individual basis was Franklin D. Roosevelt in 1932. Taking advantage of the novelty of phonograph records, FDR recorded a message of greeting and a request for support, and sent a record to each one of the delegates. In recent closely contested conventions, leading candidates have assembled card files on all of the delegates, listing all known information about

In 1960 John F. Kennedy campaigned strongly for his party's nomination months before the national convention. He entered presidential
primary contests and met many thousands of people throughout the
country.

them, their candidate preferences, the prospects of winning their
votes, and who can be most persuasive with them.

The cost of the nationwide effort needed to win a contested
nomination can run to 2 or 3 million dollars. In 1960, Hubert
Humphrey's campaign funds were totally exhausted when he with-
drew as a contender for the Democratic presidential nomination
after losing the West Virginia primary to Kennedy. This raises the
serious question of whether our presidential candidates should be
drawn only from a group of men able to raise large amounts of
campaign funds.

Reform the Process?　Many observers want the national conventions abandoned, or at least reformed to give the voters a more
direct voice in the selection of presidential candidates. Some suggest a national primary to select the candidates. Others prefer more

George Romney has projected himself into the national spotlight by his successive gubernatorial victories in Michigan. However, the road to winning the party nomination for President is a long hard one and will take a great deal of planning.

presidential primaries in the states under rules binding the delegates to support the primary winner. Most people working in politics, however, prefer the national convention. They find it a delicate device that measures both the voters' sentiments and the politicians' instincts before selecting candidates for our greatest elective office. It is a noisy, raucous affair, but it has produced a remarkably high number of able men, and most of the winners have gone on to become good and even great Presidents.

7

CAMPAIGNING:
THE CANDIDATE

Campaigns are the pitched battles of politics. For brief periods of time — usually the two months from Labor Day to Election Day — the democratic process goes through its most intensive phase: the candidates' direct appeal to the people for their votes.

A political campaign is a kaleidoscope of activity. It is excitement and long hours, enthusiasm and despair, high hopes and disappointments, exhiliration and exhaustion. But all the fanfare and confusion cannot obscure one simple, unyielding fact: the candidate is before the voters, to be watched and heard, liked or disliked, cheered or booed, respected or reviled, and, finally, approved or rejected. For all the trappings of a campaign, nothing really comes between the candidate and the voters. They see him as he is. They learn of his record. They measure his personal qualities. They assess his stands on the issues. They form the basic judgment to be made in a democratic society — whether they want this man to represent them in public office.

For the candidate the campaign is the acid test. He is on display. Every speech, every word can help or hurt his cause. Besieged on all sides to express opinions on every issue, he knows he will please some groups and, surely, lose the support of others. A series of judgments confront him, testing his intellect — and his integrity. He must first decide his position on all the current issues. On many questions the answer is easy: he has expressed his view repeatedly in the past, and his position in speeches or votes is a matter of public record. Some questions are put to him for the first time, and he must conscientiously find out all he can about them before he can honestly make up his mind.

Popular vs. Personal Decisions. Inevitably, he faces some issues where there is a conflict between what he personally believes and what position he feels the voters desire. Most candidates and office-holders stoutly claim that they always resolve issues on the basis of their personal views and beliefs. Many observers cynically charge that politicians take whatever positions they believe will be most appealing to the voters.

No candidate can preserve his self-respect nor maintain the confidence of the voters if he flops about on all the issues, taking whatever side seems popular at the moment. The voters expect a candidate to use his personal judgment. They want to see some evidence that he has a mind of his own and the capacity for creative thought. Yet even the most independent-minded candidate realizes that on some issues he must take into account the wishes of his constituency if he is to have any chance of winning election. He seeks election in a democratic society to *represent* the people, and he is properly concerned with their views so that he may in fact be their representative.

In practice the candidate steers a middle course, whether or not he admits it to himself. He does take some positions simply because they are popular with the voters. Yet he takes many more positions because he personally believes they are right. What he does when an issue presents a clear conflict between the voters' views and his own tests his mettle as a man. Some give in to popular pressure and are elected. Some maintain their convictions and are defeated. In the long run, the candidates who take their positions independently and express their views forcefully and fearlessly commend themselves to the voters. Keeping one's self-respect is a large part of winning and holding public office.

Physical and Emotional Strain.   The campaign tests more than the candidate's mind and conscience. It tests his physical and emotional stamina. Campaigns are hard work, grueling tests of endurance. The physical strain is apparent to anyone who has watched a candidate maintain the hectic pace of a campaign schedule. In England, a candidate "stands" for election. In the United States, he "runs."

The emotional strain is no less wearing. Few activities in life involve such an all-or-nothing outcome as an election, climaxing a long period of hard work and tension. Throughout the campaign, the candidate is alternately bouyed up and let down. An enthusi-

The physical and emotional strain which results from the long and strenuous campaigns takes its effect upon the candidates in the closing hours of the race.

astic crowd one day peps up his spirits. A savage editorial attack dismays him the next. A poll shows him ahead. Precinct workers report he is losing ground. So it goes day after day.

Never knowing for sure whether all his activity is winning votes or losing them, he presses on each day, doing everything he can to persuade one more person to give him a vote. He goes all day and well into the night, speaking, walking, driving, looking, listening, meeting, greeting, and more speaking. Then, suddenly, election day arrives, and it is all over. His world stops for the first time in many months. His campaign, his effort to persuade the people that he should be elected to office, comes to an end. The decision lies with the voters.

What We Don't Know. For all the importance of campaigning, we know very little about it. We know what the candidates do. But we have hardly any idea what persuades a voter to support one candidate over another. Was it a dramatic speech? A television broadcast? Eye-catching billboards? Hard-hitting newspaper ads? An attack on his opponent's voting record? A pledge to reduce taxes? It might have been one of these or all of these. Or it might have been the candidate's personality, or his firm handshake outside a factory gate, or a favor done 10 years ago, or the recommendation by the local newspaper, or the urging of a friend just as the voter walked up to the polling booth.

What the politicians don't know, they make up for by political instinct. Perhaps no important activity in American life depends so heavily on guesswork as political campaigning. Sometimes the guesses are educated, as when large sums are spent on polls to find out how the voters are reacting to campaign issues. Usually the guesses are just that—though made by men and women whose experience and insight give their guesses a high degree of reliability.

Two Basic Campaigning Rules. One popular rule of campaigning states: do again what has worked before. The candidate who ran a series of newspaper ads during his first successful campaign invariably does so in every campaign from then on. In state and national campaigns, one city often becomes the traditional site for the opening of a campaign, another for the election eve speech.

The other basic rule: try everything. Since no one knows for sure what produces a vote, it takes a brave, or foolhardy, candidate to reject out of hand some new technique for reaching the voters. Funds, of course, limit what can be done in a campaign. But within the limit of available money, the candidates try everything. What John Wanamaker said about advertising is especially true of political campaigning: "Half of everything we spend is wasted, but we don't know which half."

Starting in a Hurry. The seasonal nature of the work contributes to the hectic nature of campaigning. Most business activity runs on from year to year. The Christmas rush is planned for months in advance. But the business of winning votes operates like no other business. The party organizations try to maintain some year-round continuity. But a campaign cannot be planned until the candidates are known—often just a few months before the election. So almost all campaign activity must begin from scratch, but hit high gear in a hurry. Office space must be rented, staff hired, telephones installed, schedules made, literature printed, and money raised. Inevitably there is waste, confusion, and sometimes real chaos.

Advantage of the Incumbent. Almost half of all candidates escape much of the hurry-up nature of campaigning. These are the officeholders seeking re-election. The campaign offers these incumbents several advantages not enjoyed by their opponents.

First, they usually can count on renomination; so they can plan their campaign far in advance. One or more terms in office have made them known to the voters. They have a record to run on. They have been helpful to their constituents in ways that will be remembered at the polls. Most voters will forever support the Congressman who helped secure their social security payments or arranged for their relatives to immigrate to this country.

Incumbents also have tangible advantages — an office, a telephone, and a secretary. If his position is Congressman or Senator, the incumbent has several staff members and unlimited mailing privileges.[1] The incumbent also has greater access to the news media. As an officeholder, what he does and says makes news.

All of these advantages are magnified manyfold when the office is the Presidency. The President so dominates public attention that he starts out his campaign with a large lead over his challenger, regardless of party, time, or events. In this century, only two incumbent Presidents were denied re-election: William Howard Taft, who faced a three-way race in 1912 when Teddy Roosevelt split the Republicans, and Herbert Hoover, who faced the aftermath of the economic collapse of 1929. The odds are always with the incumbent, as Teddy Roosevelt, Woodrow Wilson, Calvin Coolidge, Franklin D. Roosevelt, Harry Truman, Dwight Eisenhower, and Lyndon Johnson have proved.

STRATEGY

Each candidate's strategy depends on who he is and what office he seeks. No sure formula works well for all candidates. Each must decide what makes sense for him, what is natural for him to do, because no candidate can convincingly be something other than himself.

The office sought determines the basic outlines of strategy. If the

---

[1] The franking privilege may not be used for purely political matters. But free postage is available for mailing all sorts of material, informing voters in a favorable way what their Congressman or Senator has been doing in Washington.

candidate is vying with 30 contenders for a place on a nine-man city council, his strategy is simple: use every possible means to get his name known to the voters. With so many candidates running, the ones who succeed in getting their names known will usually win. In two-man contests, however, especially for higher offices, a better-known name is not enough. Here the strategy has to include making the voters aware of the candidate's background, his experience, his record, his views, and his pledges of future action.

Often a candidate never formally develops a campaign strategy. Once nominated, he is on a treadmill of activity, running hard just to keep even with the demands on his time. Rarely does he enjoy the luxury of a quiet discussion with close advisors to develop strategy in a rational way. More often he starts off in a hurry to make his first speech and stays busy until election eve, making decisions on a day to day basis.

Still, some points of basic strategy must be agreed upon in every campaign. A candidate must take stock of himself and decide what he considers his strong points, what he wants to convey to the voters. It may be a highlight of his previous experience, or a legislative accomplishment, or a specific proposal for the future. One Congressman from New York, for example, manages to get into almost every campaign speech a pledge to support his pet idea — a national lottery.

In recent years many candidates have used public opinion polls to help them determine which issues they should emphasize and which are their strong and weak points with the voters. Such polls do far more than tell the candidate whether he is ahead or behind. They often supply him with useful insight into voter-opinion, and an analysis of this information suggests campaign strategies that he may have overlooked.

Campaign Style. Basic decisions must be made as to the style of the campaign. Will it be affirmative or negative? Will it concentrate on the candidate's merits or the opponent's shortcomings? Some candidates make it a point never to mention or even refer to their opponent throughout a campaign. Others, usually those challenging incumbents, often hit hardest at something their opponent has done or failed to do.

High Road or Low Road. The level of campaigning is a

crucial issue for the candidate. Almost all candidates in America disdain smear tactics. But smears have occurred, generally perpetrated by unauthorized supporters of one candidate or anonymous enemies of his opponent. False rumors whispered in every presidential campaign have impugned both major party candidates. In a Senate campaign in 1952, Senator Millard Tydings, of Maryland, was smeared by a fake photograph showing him in apparent close conversation with a well-known Communist leader. The photo was a composite of two separate photographs, fraudulently put together to look like one picture of the two men talking to each other.

Partisanship. Another key strategic decision concerns the degree of partisanship in the campaign. In recent years many candidates have shied away from close identification with their own political party. They prefer to strike a nonpartisan stance, which they hope will have greater appeal to voters in the opposing party. This happens most frequently when local election and registration figures show that one candidate's party is a distinct minority. In such circumstances, a candidate will often avoid any mention of his party affiliation in all his campaign literature and advertising. His campaign speeches will specifically urge voters to vote for the man, not the party. Many Democrats ran this way in 1956 to counter Eisenhower's popularity, as did many Republicans facing the Johnson landslide of 1964. In 1965, Republican John V. Lindsay ran for Mayor of New York City, where Democrats outnumber Republicans about three to one. He cast off his party label, pledged a nonpartisan city administration, and won!

Even candidates of a party with a local majority frequently play down partisan appeals to lure voters from the opposite party. Understandably, the candidate assumes he will have strong support from members of his own party; he sees extra votes to be won from the ranks of the opposition. Inevitably, this strategy tends to blur the differences between the parties on major issues. It is difficult for the public to see where the parties differ, as more and more candidates sharpen only the individual differences between themselves and their opponents.

Special Groups. Appeals to specific groups of voters call for special strategies. Especially in statewide and national campaigns, candidates can identify groups of voters by job or profession, ethnic

Although large metropolitan areas usually tend to favor the Democratic Party candidates, Republican John V. Lindsay was able to win the mayoralty race in New York City by running on a nonpartisan platform.

origin, or neighborhood. A mass mailing may go to all the farmers of a state, or all members of labor unions or manufacturers' associations.

Often a special group is primarily interested in a single campaign issue. Within a town or city, residents of one area want to know how the local candidates stand on building a neighborhood playground. The fishing enthusiasts of a state are concerned with the gubernatorial candidates' interest in stocking lakes and streams. Farmers look carefully at the congressional candidates' views on price-support legislation. Teachers check to see whether the nominees for President think Federal funds should be spent to increase their salaries. All of these voters pay attention to the total campaign, but the candidate who can persuade them that he will accomplish an objective they specially favor stands a good chance of winning many extra votes.

Timing.   There are two schools of thought about a final strategy decision: the timing of a campaign. One holds that a campaign should start gradually and reach a peak just before the election. The other believes most voter-decisions are made early in a campaign; so the opening stages of the battle should be the most intensive.

Election studies support both points of view. Many voters do make their decisions just after the nomination of candidates. Yet some voters reach no decision until just days before the election. The safest rule for a candidate is start early, work hard every day, and keep working until the polls close election night.

TECHNIQUES OF CAMPAIGNING

Go directly to the voter—that is the essential technique of every campaign. Aldermen and mayors, Senators and Presidents have repeatedly learned that there is no substitute for meeting the voters in person.

The people want to see their public officials. Nothing else so quickly forms their impression of the man they are asked to vote for as that one brief moment during the campaign when they see and hear him and, better still, meet him. It may be only a brief hand-shake, a quick greeting, a hurried answer to a question, but those moments often fix an impression of the candidate in a voter's mind for the entire campaign.

Meeting the Voters.   So the candidate goes forth to meet the voters, looking for them in every place imaginable. Sometimes he walks door-to-door along a quiet residential street. Or he stands at busy shopping centers, greeting the crowds as they swirl by. He shows up at a factory gate as the morning shift comes on duty at 7 a.m. He strides quickly down an assembly line, startling factory workers who never thought they would ever see a Congress-man or Senator right there in their shop. He finds commuters on the station platform in the early morning, secretaries in an office building cafeteria at noon, and retired people at a community center in the afternoon. Even a candidate for President, with a constituency of 70,000,000, wants to meet voters individually and shake their hands every chance he gets.

Steve Schapiro from Black Star

A candidate's success very often depends on getting his message across to the people. He must go out and meet the voters. He cannot wait for them to come to him. Senator Robert Kennedy has mastered this political technique.

Often the candidate leaves with each voter some reminder of their meeting. It may be just a piece of literature or a card with the candidate's name and picture. Sometimes it is a household item with the candidate's name, something that hopefully will not be thrown away, such as a calendar, ruler, pencil, book of matches, comb, or a toothbrush.

A candidate may personally meet several hundred voters in a single day, over 100,000 in a campaign. But with Congressional Districts averaging 200,000 voters and statewide campaigns reaching up to 7 million voters, few candidates can hope to meet more than a small fraction of their electorate. Why, then, do candidates make such a strenuous and time-consuming effort to reach such a small portion of the voters?

There are several reasons. First of all, the few voters whom the candidate does manage to meet will tell many of the others. Most voters do not expect to shake hands and chat with any candidate. When they do, especially if he is a major officeholder, it is an event they long remember. They tell their family, their friends, their fellow workers who, in turn, generate discussion about the candidate and remind a large number of voters that the candidate is waging an energetic campaign. Finally, the candidate benefits when he hears directly from the voters what is on their minds. When the same question or comment comes from many voters during a busy day of campaigning, he quickly learns first-hand what interests them and what issues are important to them. It may not be the issue he thought was important, but it is the issue he better talk about if he hopes to win.

Campaign Speeches.   Since the candidate knows he cannot meet more than a small fraction of the voters individually, he must get his message to them in large groups. The campaign speech is still the standard communication of every campaign.

The candidate may face 25,000 cheering supporters in a football stadium, or 25 quiet skeptics in a friend's living room. He may confront 100 silent faces at a nonpartisan luncheon, or 1,000 screaming partisans at a torchlight rally. He speaks from any available platform—the courthouse steps, a high school auditorium, the tailgate of a truck, the rear platform of a train.

The scene may be a street-corner rally in a bustling city, or a plowing contest on peaceful farmland. Often the audience includes loyal supporters, but all candidates try to find speaking opportunities before nonpartisan audiences—forums sponsored by the League of Women Voters, businessmen's luncheons, or college assemblies.

For a presidential candidate, speaking to crowds becomes an unbelievably exhausting ordeal. In 1896, William Jennings Bryan set the pattern for stumping the entire nation. He traveled 18,000 miles to deliver hundreds of speeches. Since then, most presidential candidates have followed his example. In the 1960's, candidates used jet planes to carry their campaigns into half a dozen states in a single day. In 1960, Richard Nixon became the first presidential candidate to campaign, personally, in each of the 50 states.

Such campaigning used to be stoutly resisted. In 1900, while Bryan was again rushing all over the nation, President William McKinley sat contentedly on his front porch in Canton, Ohio. He spoke only to the groups of voters that his shrewd campaign manager, Mark Hanna, arranged to travel to his home. In 1916, President Woodrow Wilson gave most of his campaign speeches to small crowds, on Saturday afternoons, at his "Shadow Lawn" home in New Jersey. In 1920, Warren G. Harding also ran a successful "front porch" campaign, and Calvin Coolidge ran his 1924 campaign without a single partisan speech. But ever since 1928, the accepted custom for presidential candidates has been to conduct a vigorous, tiring campaign trip, covering thousands of miles across the length and breadth of the nation.

Newspapers. The crowds that hear the speeches are only a small part of the vast number of voters the candidate must somehow reach with his campaign. To reach the others, he must rely on the mass media of communications — newspapers, radio, and television. In most parts of the country, the press has moved a long way from the days when a paper reported in its news columns only the speeches and activities of the candidate it supported on its editorial page. Most newspapers now take special care to give equal amounts of news space to both candidates in a campaign. Many papers also invite the candidates to write their views on leading issues, and print their statements, often side by side, shortly before the election.

Campaign coverage varies tremendously, however, from one newspaper to another. Generally, only the presidential campaign can consistently command prominent attention on news pages. In most papers, even the senate and congressional campaigns are rarely, if ever, front page news. A city campaign, involving personalities well known to the local community, will often receive major newspaper attention, including large headlines and photographs. While all candidates try hard to have the papers report their speeches and campaign activities, few believe that such articles determine an election victory.

On the editorial page, most papers exercise their rights to endorse particular candidates. Sometimes a paper will content itself with just a single editorial, expressing its preference. Other papers not only endorse a candidate, but keep up a drumfire attack on his opponent, with a series of editorials throughout the campaign. Most of the newspapers in this country generally support candidates of the Republican Party, though, in 1964, President Johnson became the first Democratic presidential candidate to win the editorial support of more newspapers than his Republican opponent.

Radio and TV. Radio and, later, television opened unprecedented opportunities for candidates to bring their campaigns to large numbers of voters. In 1924, the presidential candidates began to use radio, and it continued through the years to be the single most effective way to reach large numbers of voters, until television began to rival it in 1948.

Most politicians would agree that President Franklin D. Roosevelt was the most skillful radio campaigner. In his 1932 campaign and during his Presidency, he spoke to the Nation in broadcasts he called "fireside chats." His firm, confident voice became familiar to millions of voters, and brought a winning impression of FDR directly into their homes.

By 1952, television had become the most valuable way to reach masses of voters. At first, candidates used the new medium to make campaign speeches directly to the viewing audience at home. It soon became apparent, however, that a half-hour speech could not compete for the viewer's attention with the popular entertainment shows on other channels.

Candidates reacted in two ways. First, many abandoned the full-length campaign speech in favor of brief five-minute messages that could be conveniently scheduled at the end of a regular program. Then, many candidates began to vary the format of their programs. Some used documentary films illustrating their records and accomplishments. Others were shown being asked questions by passers-by on a street corner. In 1964, Senator Goldwater used a half-hour of television time for an informal chat with General Eisenhower at his Gettysburg Farm. President Johnson invited a group of young people to visit the White House and ask him informal questions before the TV cameras.

Some candidates use a "telethon" program, lasting an hour or more, inviting the viewing audience to telephone questions to them at the television studio. Seated in front of a score of attractive young ladies answering the telephones, the candidate takes the questions as they come and answers them. Spontaneity adds to the interest of the program. Richard Nixon used this device for several hours on television, the day before the 1960 election.

Perhaps the most dramatic campaign telecast by a national candidate was Richard Nixon's speech in the 1952 campaign. Running for Vice-President on the same ticket with General Eisenhower, Nixon was sharply criticized for paying the expenses of his Senate office and his campaign from a fund set up by California businessmen. The attack threatened to become a major political liability. There was speculation that Eisenhower might even drop Nixon from the ticket.

Responding to this crisis, Nixon appeared on television with his attractive wife, two young daughters, and the family dog, "Checkers." With deep feeling, he described his humble background and the financial burdens of his family. He met the fund issue head-on, describing what expenses had been paid, by whom, and who kept the records. The speech was a masterful statement of personal honesty.

Democrats dismissed the speech as "corny," but the political impact was successful. Eisenhower hailed the candid and forthright explanation, the public showered Nixon with favorable letters and telegrams, and the issue almost entirely dropped out of the campaign. The "Checkers Speech" had carried the day.

Television has given new significance to an historical campaign technique: the face-to-face debate between rival candidates. Abraham Lincoln and Stephen A. Douglas held the best-known series of such debates in their battle for a U. S. Senate seat in 1858.

A century later, in 1960, John F. Kennedy and Richard Nixon engaged in a series of four televised debates that were seen by an estimated 90 million people! While the TV-debates were not repeated by the presidential candidates in 1964, they did set a pattern followed in many campaigns for national and local offices throughout the country. Since 1960, hundreds of candidates for the U. S. Senate and the House, for Governor, and for mayor have met their opponents in televised debates. Nowadays, the failure of a candidate to accept his opponent's challenge to debate becomes a major campaign issue.

Campaign Activity. Most candidates supplement their speech-making with various types of activity that will impress the voters with their capacity to be effective officeholders. Incumbents have all sorts of ready-made opportunities to carry on the duties of their office during a campaign and to let the voters know what they are doing. Elected officials often arrange for some popular government action — opening a new school or highway — to happen close to the time they seek re-election.

Presidential activity, triggered by world events without any planned connection to a political campaign, nevertheless has an overwhelming impact on voters. On the weekend before the 1956 election, the threat of war in the Middle East focused the attention of every voter on the White House. President Eisenhower assured the nation that the United States would urge the United Nations to bring about a cease-fire and the withdrawal of the invaders. Early in the 1964 campaign, President Johnson won public support in many quarters after he promptly dispatched warplanes to bomb bases in North Vietnam, from which an attack had been launched on U. S. ships. Generally, such international events rally popular opinion behind a President, regardless of party.

Dramatic actions at home can also have a major bearing on a political campaign. In the closing days of the 1960 campaign, the Negro civil rights leader, Martin Luther King, Jr., was arrested and jailed in Atlanta. John Kennedy telephoned Dr. King's wife to express his concern and offer help. Many believe that this incident, widely reported throughout the Nation, contributed to the strong vote Kennedy received in most Negro voting districts.

A Typical Day. The full range of a candidate's activity is limited only by his own imagination and endurance. The campaign trail is long and exhausting. The days are long, the meals are rarely on schedule, and sleep is scarce.

For a senatorial candidate a typical day might run something like this. Up at 5:30 a.m. to meet the early shift coming to work at a steel plant; a breakfast meeting with party leaders of an important community in his state; morning coffee hours in several homes where friends have invited their neighbors to meet the candidate; a luncheon speech to a local Rotary Club; a quick stop at campaign headquarters to check schedule for the coming week and approve press

In an effort to meet as many voters as possible, the campaign caravan will carry the candidate, often accompanied by his family, throughout the areas in which he seeks election.

releases; a tour of stores in a suburban shopping plaza; a brief stop at the television studio to make video tapes of one-minute telecasts to be shown during the final week of the campaign; an hour's drive to meet key labor leaders who want to ask the candidate for his views on domestic issues; a tour of a home for the aged; drive back to a reception sponsored by the party organization in another city (the drive back provides a few moments to dictate remarks for evening speech); interviews by newspaper reporters in the city where the main evening speech will be made; a quick stop at a testimonial dinner for a retiring school board president; a dinner and speech at a downtown hotel; brief appearances at two ward meetings and a Congressional District rally; final stop, at a dance sponsored by young party workers; then, home and into bed at 12:30 a.m., with just a few moments to take a look at tomorrow's back-breaking schedule.

PUBLICITY

Slogans. In all campaigns, major efforts are made to use all the

In some cases a campaign advertisement can be used to the advantage of the opposition. Note the additional banner placed below the billboard for Senator Goldwater.

techniques of publicity and advertising. The oldest, simplest, and often the most effective device is the slogan. Few voters forget Harding's "Back to Normalcy," "Keep Cool with Coolidge," Hoover's "Two Chickens in Every Pot," Franklin Roosevelt's "New Deal," Truman's "Fair Deal," Eisenhower's "Great Crusade," Kennedy's "New Frontier," and Johnson's "Great Society."

Sometimes a single remark becomes the key phrase in a campaign. In 1952, with the prolonged fighting in Korea weighing on the American voters, Eisenhower captured the public's imagination with his ringing declaration "I shall go to Korea."

Occasionally, one phrase can turn out to be a campaign's major liability, as James G. Blaine, the Republican presidential nominee, found out in his 1884 campaign against Grover Cleveland. Arriving for a speech in New York, Blaine was greeted by a clergyman who branded the Democrats as "the party whose antecedents have been rum, Romanism and rebellion." These last four words were picked up by Democratic leaders who reminded their followers, over and over again, of this unfortunate Republican attack. Catholic Democrats were infuriated; Blaine lost New York and with it a close election.

Political campaigners often put their own twist on the opposition's political slogans. In 1964, Goldwater ads and billboards featured the slogan "In your heart you know he's right." To underscore Goldwater's identification with some right-wing supporters, Democrats added one word with this result: "In your heart you know he's far right." Or poking fun at some of Goldwater's more extreme proposals, they countered with a slogan of their own: "In your heart you know he might."

Literature. Campaign literature has been distributed in great quantity throughout the history of American politics. In earlier days, speeches were the principal item reprinted. Millions of copies of a presidential candidate's acceptance speech were distributed throughout the country.

Today, pamphlets with pictures and text tell about the candidate's background and give reasons for supporting him. A more recent innovation has been the use of comic books, telling the candidate's story in a simple, direct fashion.

In every election year, hundreds of millions of pieces of literature are printed on behalf of candidates for all offices. Invariably, a large portion of this literature never reaches the voters. Printed late in the campaign and shipped to party workers too busy to arrange for house-to-house distribution, much of it ends up in the basement of local campaign headquarters.

One way to make sure that campaign messages reach the homes of the voters is to send them through the mails, though the costs are high. Sometimes different campaign leaflets are designed for special mailing lists—teachers, doctors, farmers, or members of a labor union. In many campaigns the candidate sends a letter or post card to all registered voters asking them directly for their vote.

Campaign Ads. Most campaigns use some or all of the traditional forms of political advertising—buttons; bumper strips for cars; newspaper ads; ads on busses, in train stations, and in subways; posters; billboards; and spot announcements on radio and television. In local and state campaigns, thousands of dollars are spent for such items. In national campaigns, the cost runs into the millions.

"Selling" a Candidate. This type of massive advertising raises the question of whether a political candidate can be "sold" to the public like soap or breakfast food. Some advertising men think the answer is "yes." Most successful politicians are sure the answer is "no." Skilled propagandists can persuade people that one bar of soap or one cereal is better than others. But the act of voting is quite different from the act of purchasing. The voters are making up their minds whom they want in public office. They form a total impression of the man based on everything they know about him. Traditional advertising techniques can help to publicize a candidate's name and some favorable things about him. But no amount of advertising or public relations can manufacture a favorable impression of an unimpressive candidate.

Voters use a basic common sense that is not always present in their choice of supermarket products. Despite all the fanfare and clamor of campaigning, the voters assess the candidate himself —unvarnished by any gloss of publicity. They take a man on his merit, judge him for what he is, and render their verdict in the privacy of the polling booth. Over the years, the voters' record of sound judgment has been remarkably good.

8

CAMPAIGNING: PARTISANS AND CITIZENS

The candidate is the key to the campaign. His failings lead to defeat. His strengths make victory possible. Yet no candidate can win public office without the campaign activity of other people — perhaps a handful in a local contest, millions in a national election. From the campaign manager to the volunteer who stuffs envelopes, each campaigner plays a vital part in the political process. And all are needed if the candidate is to win.

These armies of political workers include people of diverse talents, experience, and motives. They are lawyers, housewives, students, businessmen, workingmen, people of all ages from all backgrounds with all kinds of experience; the seasoned political "pros" who have been involved in campaigns for all of their adult lives, and the novices with no campaign experience at all.

Some of these men and women leave their regular jobs to campaign full-time for 2 or 3 months. Others devote 2 or 3 hours most evenings every week of the campaign. Many stop by campaign headquarters to volunteer for 1 hour a week, glad to help out with whatever chores need doing. Some have high ideals they want to advance. Others have suddenly become excited over a single issue — the need for a new school, or a treaty to end nuclear testing. Some seek only personal rewards of prestige, a job, or money.

One common fact unites them: the political bug has bitten them all. Each has succumbed to the fascination of politics. Each seeks the thrill of direct participation in the larger-than-life world of politics. Each finds the satisfaction of affecting the outcome in some way, large or small.

THE CANDIDATE'S CAMPAIGNERS

The Campaign Manager.   In the group of people working directly for the candidate, there is always one person, besides the candidate himself, who makes the central decisions of the campaign. He may be known as the campaign manager, the campaign director, or he may have no formal designation whatever. The title does not matter, but the man does. William McKinley had Mark Hanna; Franklin D. Roosevelt had James A. Farley; John F. Kennedy had his brother, Robert.

To the campaign manager fall the myriad tasks of setting up the campaign, keeping it moving, and leaving the candidate as free as possible to concentrate on his major task—winning votes. In a national campaign, the manager is the top executive, running a campaign organization of hundreds of people. In a local election, he is a do-it-yourself man, writing press releases, renting a hall, printing posters, driving the candidate to an evening rally, placing political advertisements in the newspaper, and ordering campaign buttons.

He is coach of a team, jockey to a high-strung thoroughbred, concertmaster to the supreme prima donna—the political candidate. It is his job to tell the candidate the blunt truths that others hide from him. He cautions the candidate when wild schemes are suggested. He keeps the candidate and all the workers rooted to the campaign's basic themes and objectives, especially when the heat of partisan conflict tempts many to branch out recklessly toward foolish pitfalls.

Writers, Researchers, and Planners.   Close to the candidate are several skilled people handling necessary behind-the-scenes work.

Even though most campaign speeches are given "off the cuff," there are times during a campaign that require a prepared speech. It is physically impossible for a candidate in a statewide or national campaign to find the time to write every speech himself. The candidate's staff may include a speechwriter, or college professors and other experts who may supply speech material in their specialized fields. A newspaperman or someone with experience in journalism writes press releases that tell local reporters what the candidate is doing and what he plans to say in his speeches. Skillful campaign speech writers often become key aides to elected officials: Theodore Sorensen and Arthur Schlesinger, Jr., with President Kennedy; Bill Moyers and Jack Valenti with President Johnson. The candidate's press secretary usually continues in this role after a successful election: James Hagerty with President Eisenhower and Pierre Salinger with President Kennedy.

Research must be done so that the candidate has the facts and figures to back up the points he wants to make. When a candidate runs against an incumbent Congressman or Senator, a staff member checks the entire voting record of the opponent and everything he ever said in debate on the floor of Congress. In his successful 1964 U. S. Senate campaign, Robert Kennedy put Senator Kenneth Keating on the defensive, with a series of newspaper ads, documenting the Senator's votes against legislation Kennedy favored.

Scheduling becomes a major job in a statewide campaign. Someone must arrange the candidate's schedule of speeches, rallies, and coffee hours in neighbors' homes. Hopefully, a series of engagements in one part of the state will be scheduled on the same day so that valuable time will not be wasted driving long distances. This staff member also has to fend off hundreds of requests from local groups demanding that the candidate appear at their rallies on just the night he has agreed to be somewhere else.

In modern national campaigns, planning the candidate's itinerary has become a full-time job for dozens of campaign staff members. "Advance men" arrive 2 weeks ahead of the candidate in each city he will visit. There, they make all the necessary arrangements — securing hotel rooms, arranging TV interviews, planning parade routes, even arbitrating disputes over which local politicians will have a place on the rostrum when the candidate makes his major speech.

Another campaign chore is arranging for prominent speakers to visit the states to lend their support to local and statewide candidates. Congressmen, Senators, Governors, and Cabinet members travel across the country during the campaign season, speaking for their party's candidates. The appearance of a well-known national figure in a local candidate's hometown wins major coverage in the local press and on television.

Fund Raising. Raising money for the candidate has become a major task. The costs of campaigning rise every year. The increased use of television in campaigns has been a big item — a half-hour of evening time on a single network costs about $75,000. Even in a local campaign the cost of a one-minute TV message may run as high as $1,750.

Congressional campaigns in contested Districts have cost from $15,000 to $200,000. Senate campaigns have cost more than $1 million. Several million dollars are spent by both sides in national campaigns. In 1964, it is estimated that total costs of all campaigns amounted to $200 million.

Where does the money come from? The candidate himself has to assume much of the burden of raising money. He is expected to pay a share of the costs himself, but even a wealthy man cannot afford more than a small part of the costs. Distasteful as it may be to him, he simply has to ask for financial help from his friends, business associates, college classmates, and any others he thinks may wish to see him succeed. Usually, he designates a finance chairman to work on raising money.

Fund raising dinners have become a successful device, with ticket prices ranging from $5 to $1,000 per person. Another technique is the "sale" of campaign emblems, with a generous profit going to the campaign fund. Appeals for contributions are sometimes mailed to millions of homes. Some candidates, on their radio and TV programs, invite contributions from the listeners. Ronald Reagan's television speech for Barry Goldwater in the 1964 presidential campaign reportedly raised $1 million from the viewers.

Traditionally, the major portion of campaign funds comes from a relatively small number of large contributions. Both parties try to encourage large numbers of their supporters to make small contributions, but this approach rarely produces much money. Former Republican National Chairman Leonard Hall has said that he never saw a national campaign where individual contributions of less than

Haynie, *Atlanta Journal*

$10 produced more than $1 million, until 1964. But in that year, an aggressive effort by Republicans to seek a large quantity of small contributions netted $6 million in individual contributions of $10 or less. Republicans also reported that there were 2 million separate contributors to their total 1964 fundraising effort, compared with the 50,000 to 80,000 contributors in previous campaigns.

Large contributions raise serious questions. While many contributors give "emotional money" because of their personal liking for a candidate or his cause, others regularly make sizable contributions to candidates of both parties without any concern for issues or ideals. Plainly, this latter group hope their contributions will make the victorious candidate more likely to do them a favor. At the very least, they want to avoid incurring his displeasure for not having contributed.

The issue becomes even more delicate when the contribution is related to the way the candidate will vote. Few candidates really make such commitments. A campaign donation for a specific promise to vote for or against a bill is a bribe, prohibited by law.

Yet, most contributors support a candidate because they believe his philosophy will cause him to vote the way they want him to vote. This is not bribery; it is giving financial support to those who will fight for what you believe. The line is clear in principle but occasionally a bit fuzzy in practice.

Most candidates are smart enough to distinguish between the good-faith contribution and the bad-faith bribe. If there is any question about the motives of the person offering the contribution, reject it. That's the simplest and safest rule.

Various laws seek to regulate campaign contributions. Some limit the amount of money an individual may contribute to a campaign (the federal limit is $5,000), but this approach is ineffective since several contributions can legally be made, each to a different committee spending funds on a candidate's behalf. Other statutes require disclosure by the candidate and his committees of all campaign contributions and expenditures, listing the names of those who gave and received the money. These reporting requirements produce information on almost all campaign funds, though often reports need not be filed until after the election.

THE PARTY'S CAMPAIGNERS

Campaign activity of both major party organizations varies from state to state and from election to election. In some places there is a strong tradition of campaigning by party workers; in others the party fulfills only housekeeping chores, leaving the task of winning votes entirely to the candidate and his personal workers.

Party Fund-raising. The parties undertake their own fund-raising activities, usually separate from the efforts made by the candidates. The party needs funds to pay the costs of headquarters, for its share of campaign activities, and for the expenses of election-day work. These funds are raised, usually, by $100-a-plate dinners and by direct mail solicitation.

Role of National Party Organizations. In recent years, the national committees of both parties have performed important tasks not only for the presidential nominees but also for congressional candidates. The national committees contract for the publicity of the presidential campaigns. They purchase network radio and television time and print literature, automobile bumper strips, and campaign buttons. Researchers prepare a campaign fact book, listing the accomplishments of the presidential nominee and of the party, their stands on all the major issues, and the principal shortcomings of the opposition.

The national committees act as service organizations for congressional candidates, helping out with campaign assistance, money, and ways of saving money. For example, the national committee of the President's party will arrange for all the Senate and House candidates of his party to come to Washington and have photographs and motion picture film clips made of each candidate with the President. Back home the local candidate then uses this film in an effective TV commercial. The President is seen in intimate conversation with the candidate, while an announcer quotes the President's urgent plea that the local candidate be elected to Congress.

Both national committees and the campaign committees, which each party runs for Senate and House candidates, give money directly to these candidates in their state contests. These contributions may range from a few hundred dollars in a House contest to as much as $25,000 in a major Senate race.

The national offices try to save money for local candidates by preparing campaign materials for them. For example, they distribute to congressional candidates a 45-second television film, giving a highlight of the career of the presidential nominee or illustrating an issue in the campaign. The local candidate simply adds his own message to the end of these films, thus producing a professionally made 1-minute commercial for a fraction of the usual cost.

Role of State Party Organizations. State party organizations often take no direct part in the campaign activities of U. S. Senate and House candidates. These organizations devote major attention to a contest for Governor, because control of the state house can aid the continued strength of their parties. Governors can make hundreds, and in some states thousands, of politically helpful appointments. Senators and Congressmen have little patronage to dispense. In almost every state, the party would rather risk the loss of all its representatives in the Senate and the House than have its candidate be defeated for Governor. Yet, even gubernatorial campaigns are sometimes run independently of the party organization, most often when the candidate for Governor has won the nomination in a bitter fight against the organization's choice.

If a state party organization chooses to play an active campaign role, generally, its activities parallel what the national committees do for the presidential candidates. Workers, funds, and publicity are the major areas of assistance. Of course, all candidates find it helpful to have their party organization working solidly for their victory.

Voter Registration. A state organization concentrates its activity on voter-registration, voter-turnout, and other jobs that must be done in every campaign no matter who is running. Tactics vary widely throughout the country, but almost all state organizations make some effort to add to the voter lists every person they think may support candidates of their party.

The Democrats of Mercer County (Trenton), New Jersey, conduct one of the most successful party-registration efforts. During the 1940's, this county moved out of the Republican column and over to the Democratic side largely through an intensive voter-registration drive. The technique is simple. In the late afternoon and early evening hours of each day when new voters can be registered, teams of party workers stream through all neighborhoods, knocking at the door of every house and apartment. They inquire if anyone in the household is not registered. Often they find a family which has moved from another state within the past year, a young man just turned 21, an elderly mother-in-law who has moved in with her family. Unless the party workers conclude from the conversation that the unregistered person is plainly a Republican, they make an intensive effort to take him, right then, to the appropriate officials to be registered. Other workers on the team are knocking on doors of homes across the street, and workers' cars are on the street, ready to drive the new voters to be registered. The air of excitement usually overcomes any reluctance to accept the invitation. If the prospective voter positively cannot leave home at that time, a firm date is made to return and bring him to be registered at another time. Before the registration period is over, every home and apartment have been covered.

One of the keys to party success in any election is the ability to encourage large voter registrations. If you can convince a person to vote, you can probably convince him that he should vote for you or your party.

Few communities organize their registration drive this well, but something approaching this procedure is usually done. Workers may canvass at least those areas where the party generally runs well. Or if house calls cannot be made, an intensive telephone campaign is organized to remind people when they can become registered and to offer rides if needed.

In this way party workers add thousands of voters to the rolls each election year in many areas. In some elections, the extra number of voters added to the lists in such registration drives made the difference between victory and defeat.

Absentee Ballots.   Party workers also make sure that voters who will be unable to get to the polls on election day vote beforehand by absentee ballot. The laws of the states vary on who is eligible to vote by absentee ballot. Usually, those registered voters who, on election day, will be out of the state, or in the armed forces, or confined to a hospital or nursing home can vote without appearing at the polls. These voters may apply for an absentee

United Press International Photo

Absentee ballots are available for many eligible voters who may be unable to reach the polls on election day. Many of our servicemen, even in the midst of warfare, have found the time to cast their ballots before election day.

ballot, on which the names of all the candidates appear. They mark these paper ballots and return them to the election officials. On election day these absentee ballots are counted along with all the votes cast that day.

Party workers make sure that their supporters who will not be at the polls apply for their absentee ballots and mail them in before the local deadline. The party that does the better job winning absentee votes begins election day with an important headstart. In state-wide elections in the larger states more than 100,000 votes are cast by absentee ballots. How important are absentee ballots? In the 1960 presidential contest in California, Nixon won 52,727 more absentee votes than Kennedy, and carried the state by just 35,623 votes.

Door-to-Door Campaigning. Bringing the campaign personally to the voters is often an important part of the party workers' job. Where the party is well organized, party workers conduct a door-to-door canvass of an entire area, urging support of their party's candidates and, perhaps, leaving some campaign literature at each home or apartment. This canvass may be made along with the registration effort. Sometimes it is done just before election day, coupled with a reminder to vote and an offer of transportation to the polls. Often hundreds of party workers personally solicit thousands of voters by telephone.

The pattern of direct canvassing is uneven throughout the country. In some well-organized precincts, party workers contact every voter once and every party member several times. In other places, where the party organization is lazy or nonexistent, voters may not receive a single personal contact during the entire campaign. In 1964, about 12 million people of the 70 million who voted were contacted personally by party workers.

Preparing for Election Day. During the campaign period, party workers begin the all-important effort to bring out the vote on election day. Besides the house-to-house canvass, the party organization prepares itself for the work that must be done during all the hours the polls are open. In each voting district, leaders meet regularly with all their workers to assign election day jobs. Workers will be needed to drive cars, to check the voter lists to see who has not voted, to serve as poll-watchers, and to hand out literature in front of the polling places.

Putting this small army of workers into the field on election day requires careful advance preparation. In well-organized areas, workers meet with their leaders once a week to check on the progress of the campaign, to make plans, and, generally, to increase partisan enthusiasm.

In party clubhouses, restaurant backrooms, and crowded living rooms, the scene changes, but the script is always the same. The precinct captain looks sternly at his loyal band of workers and with an absolutely straight face assures them, as he has many times before, that *this* election is the most important one they have ever faced. "All the efforts of past years will be wiped out if we lose. A victory will bring us all to the edge of the promised land." High school cheerleaders could learn a good lesson from the campaign "pep talk" that precinct leaders give their workers in the final weeks before election day.

Talbot Lovering

During election campaigns party headquarters suddenly appear in various stores and homes in an area, and disappear just as quickly after the election is over.

THE CITIZEN CAMPAIGNERS

The candidate's own workers and the party's workers are the professional soldiers of the political wars. They believe in their candidate and their party. Some are paid, and many expect some reward in the form of a job or, at least, an advance upward through the party ranks. But as with most mobilization efforts, the needed reservoir of manpower must come from the citizens who join the cause simply because they believe it is a worthy one.

Each year more and more people, who have never before had anything to do with politics, enter political campaigns. Usually a presidential election stirs them into action, but it may be a hotly contested battle for a seat on the school board or a city council election. Very often the appearance of a new and attractive candidate prompts these citizen-volunteers to join the fray. The candidacies of Eisenhower, Stevenson, Kennedy, and Goldwater each brought thousands of men and women to politics for their first taste of campaigning. In 1960, an estimated 6 million citizens volunteered for political work—probably more in 1964.

The volunteers do the odd jobs, the little jobs, the jobs the "big-shots" are too busy to do– in other words, the important jobs. A high school student stops by campaign headquarters after school to stuff envelopes with the candidate's leaflet. A housewife spends 6 hours a week on the telephone, urging citizens to register. Her neighbor arranges a coffee hour for the congressional candidate and invites 40 ladies to meet him in her living room. A college student checks the voting record of the incumbent Senator the party is trying to defeat. A youngster goes door-to-door through his neighborhood, distributing a campaign leaflet. A young woman sets up a booth at a shopping center, seeking one-dollar contributions for her party. An older woman spends an afternoon a week at party headquarters, answering the telephone.

Most volunteers are women. They have the time–and they are reliable. In politics, men do most of the talking, but women do most of the work.

These citizen-workers join the campaign effort in a different way. Some come to work for individual candidates. Others volunteer their time to the party organizations. Many channel their activity into special citizens-organizations set up during every campaign.

Auxiliary Citizens-Organizations. In most state campaigns and in all national campaigns, citizens-organizations are established to enlist support from the unaffiliated voters and voters in the opposition party. Many voters are willing to work for and be publicly identified with a candidate so long as they need not be associated with his party. Usually these organizations are known as "Citizens for X" or "Volunteers for Y." Sometimes a candidate will aim his citizens-organization more pointedly at the votes he is seeking. A Democratic candidate, for example, may be supported by an organization called "Republicans and Independents for Smith."

Special citizens-groups are also established to appeal to voters on the basis of their occupation. In 1964, for example, there was a group called, "Scientists and Engineers for Johnson."

All of these groups seek to enlist other citizens to support their candidate. Branch offices, with decorated headquarters, are opened in various communities to publicize the group's support. Mass mailings are sent to potential members of the organizations, seeking votes and funds for further campaign activity. Rallies are sponsored

so that the candidate and others on his slate can speak to an audience drawn from beyond the ranks of partisan followers.
The Power of Personal Persuasion. In the final analysis, every citizen has an opportunity to participate in a campaign through his individual ability to persuade his fellow citizens. Aside from the activities of the candidate himself, the single most persuasive influence that can be brought to bear upon a voter is the individual approach of another voter. The most effective campaign is the word-of-mouth campaign. If people in a community start mentioning to each other—in factories, in offices, and over backyard fences—that Jones is a good candidate who deserves a vote, Jones is likely to win. If the person-to-person reports are adverse, the candidate is in serious trouble.

The political power of each citizen is not limited to his own vote. Each citizen has the personal capacity to influence the votes of others. The collective force of these personal persuasions is the strongest force in politics and the key to victory at the polls.

9

ELECTION

DAY

The last speech is made. The last hand is shaken. The campaign is over. Election day arrives. On this single day the fate of thousands of candidates will be decided, and, perhaps, the destiny of millions of citizens. It is the most crucial day in the life of the democratic process.

Congress has established the first Tuesday after the first Monday in November as the date for the election of candidates to National offices. On that date, the presidential elections are held every four years, and all 435 members of the House of Representatives and one-third of the U. S. Senate are elected every two years.

Most of the states also use this same November date for electing their state officials—the Governor and members of the state legislature—and many local officers. However, all the states do not elect their officials in the same year. Some fill the major state offices in the presidential election year. Others separate state elections from National elections so that state campaigns will not be influenced by presidential issues. Of the 36 states where the Governor serves a 4-year term, 24 states hold their gubernatorial elections in a non-presidential election year. Within this group, 20 hold their state elections on the even-numbered years between presidential elections, and 4 hold their elections in odd-numbered years to avoid the influence of congressional issues.

In some states, local elections—city and town—are held in the spring or early fall so that their own issues may be considered clearly, apart from the influence of the November elections for state and National offices.

Almost all elections in the United States are held on a Tuesday, unlike many other democratic nations which hold their elections on Saturday or Sunday. In some countries the polls stay open longer than a single day. In Finland an election lasts 2 days, in Italy and Switzerland, 1 1/2 days.

Each state determines the location of the polling places and the hours they are open for voting. Within each state, these decisions are often left to local authorities. Each precinct sets up its own polling place to serve the several hundred registered voters in that precinct. The voting hours vary from as few as 7 in rural Tennessee to as many as 15 in New York City. Generally, polls open at 6 or 7 a.m. and close at 6, 7, or 8 p.m.

GETTING OUT THE VOTE

For most party organizations, election day is the crucial day of the political year – and the day of hardest work. On this day the parties must make sure their supporters get to the polls. Most voters, of course, need no urging. They are eager to vote, especially in presidential elections. But in every precinct there are supporters of each major party who do not vote unless somebody contacts them and, in some cases, unless somebody transports them to the polls.

Election figures show the importance of getting out the vote. In presidential years, the few who do not vote – some 10 – 15% of the registered voters in most states – are usually more numerous than the margin between the candidates. And in local and primary elections, the eligible voters who fail to vote sometimes exceed the total votes received by the winner! In 1960, for example, Congressman Edwin E. Willis won the Democratic nomination for Congress from Louisiana's Third District with 39,516 votes out of 52,509; the number of registered Democrats who failed to vote was 101,843.

All political parties recognize the importance of bringing to the polls every last one of their supporters. Of course, neither party can be sure that every voter will support his party's candidates. But a very high percent of the membership will vote for most, if not all, of the candidates of their party. So the effort to bring party supporters to the polls goes on at full speed.

Election-day activity in well-organized precincts begins long before the day arrives. Workers are recruited for their tasks and given specific instructions. Arrangements are made to borrow or rent automobiles to take voters to the polls. Up-to-date voter lists are prepared, showing the correct addresses and telephone numbers of the party's membership in each precinct. Money is distributed to local leaders to pay party workers, in those areas where they customarily receive a day's wages for their election-day efforts. Many workers, however, serve as volunteers without pay.

When the polls open, the workers' various jobs begin. They dispatch cars to pick up voters who have asked campaign headquarters for a ride to the polls. If a mother is at home with young children, the organization sends along a babysitter to mind the children while their mother votes. Car rides are especially important for older people and for the disabled who simply cannot vote unless some provision is made to get them to the polls.

As the day wears on, party workers at the polling places carefully watch their voter lists, checking off each party supporter as he votes. By late afternoon, reports are sent back to precinct headquarters with the names of those who have not yet voted. Special efforts are made to bring these voters to the polls. In some precincts, party workers man a battery of telephones, calling those who have not yet voted and imploring them to get to the polls. In others, the party organization sends workers and cars to the homes of those who have not voted, with instructions to bring them out to vote. This activity continues up to the minute the polls close.

Party leaders insist that this effort to bring voters to the polls is vital to election victory. They spend weeks before election planning for this one day's activity. And in some parts of the country, they spend thousands of dollars to make sure the job is done.

When the candidates or the issues are provocative and challenging, voter-turnout is likely to be high regardless of party activity. But in many large cities, the percent of voter-turnout is highest where the political parties do an energetic job on election day.

AT THE POLLING PLACE

For all the majesty of the democratic process, the people usually go about the job of electing their public officials in an uninspiring place – often, a school gymnasium, a firehouse, or a police station.

A few decades ago, it was common practice to set up polling booths in stores rented for registration and election days. The payment to a neighborhood barber or grocer was a useful form of local patronage. Today most polling places are located in public buildings.

The number of polling booths in any precinct depends largely on the number of registered voters in that precinct. As a rule, enough booths are set up so that even during the peak voting hours, from the end of the workday to poll closing time, voters will not have to wait too long to cast their ballots. Each voting booth is, usually, a curtained enclosure containing a voting machine, or a shelf or flat surface on which a paper ballot may be marked.

The Secret Ballot.   Perhaps the most significant fact about an American polling place is the privacy afforded the voter in casting his ballot. The secret ballot is now an accepted and unquestioned part of American politics, yet it is a comparatively recent development.

In the early years of this country, people cast their votes by announcing their choice out loud to an election official. Later, paper ballots came into use, but these did not insure secrecy. The names of the candidates of each party were printed on separate ballots — and, often, of different colors. When the voter selected the ballot he wished to mark and dropped it into the ballot box, his choice was usually apparent to anyone watching.

Demand for secrecy at the polling place grew during the 19th century, especially after the Civil War. In 1888, the secret ballot, known as the Australian ballot, was first used in a municipal election in Louisville, Kentucky. The following year, Massachusetts approved its use in all elections. Many states had adopted the secret ballot by 1900, but it was not until 1950 that this reform was in effect in every state.

Paper Ballots and Voting Machines.   Votes are recorded on either paper ballots or voting machines. More than half the voters in presidential elections now use machines. When using a paper ballot, the voter places a mark in a small square next to the name of the candidate he favors. Some local regulations strictly require that only an X mark be used and that the mark be entirely within the square. In such localities, ballots have been ruled invalid where check marks or other symbols were used, or where the lines of the

The increasing number of voting machines which are replacing paper ballots makes the voting process much easier, the tabulation more accurate, and the results available much sooner.

X extended outside the square. After the ballot is marked, the voter places it in a locked ballot box.

To operate a voting machine, the voter first pulls a large lever that closes the curtain around himself and the machine and readies it to record votes. Then he pulls the small levers above, or next to, the names of candidates he wants to support. Finally, he pulls the large lever back to record the votes he has cast, and it simultaneously opens the curtain. The machine keeps a running total of votes cast for each candidate, which can be read off when the machine is opened after the polls close.

The newest voting innovation has been the introduction of computerized elections. In several states, the voter slips a specially designed data processing card into the voting unit so that it positions itself exactly underneath a printed ballot. The voter uses a stylus to punch holes, in the card, next to the candidate's name or the "yes" or "no" choices in a referendum. The punched card ballots are then placed in the ballot box. After the polls have closed, the punched card ballots are taken to a computer center and fed into a data processing machine which rapidly and accurately tabulates the results.

In the town of Braintree, Massachusetts, the final returns in their first computerized election, in 1966, were completely tabu-

The computer is the most recent innovation introduced into the election process. The voter marks his choices on a punch card ballot. At the close of the polls, the ballots are tabulated swiftly by a computer.

lated some 10 hours earlier than the final returns had been available the previous year when paper ballots were used. The actual computing time took 31 minutes. This new voting system could be the solution to the problems of delay, inefficiency, and the heavy costs of elections faced by most municipalities.

The Long Ballot. The most distinctive characteristic of American ballots is their length. In no other country are so many public offices filled by election. In England, for example, the ballot is the size of a postcard, with only two or three contests to be decided at each election. In this country, the ballot may contain the names of hundreds of candidates for 50 or more offices. It is a rare voter who knows the names of all the candidates running for all the offices in an American election. He usually has an opinion on the contests for President, Governor, U. S. Senator, Congressman, and mayor, but chances are he has never heard of the candidates running for county assessor, state auditor, or district judge.[1]

The Ballot Arrangement. The form of the ballot varies from

---

[1] Sometimes unknown names confront the voter casting his vote for President and Vice-President. Ballots in some states list the names of the presidential electors, people most voters never heard of. However, these ballots also include a statement indicating which presidential and vice-presidential candidates the electors will support if chosen. In other states, the ballot prominently displays the names of candidates for President and Vice-President, sometimes indicating in smaller type that electors for these candidates are technically being voted for.

one state to another, and the differences can have an important effect on the election outcome. In 33 states, all the candidates of each political party are listed in a separate row or column.[2] This party-column arrangement, known as the Indiana ballot, enables the voter to identify quickly the candidates of the political party he favors.

In the remaining 17 states, candidates are grouped according to the office they seek. One block on the ballot lists all the candidates for President and Vice President, another lists all the candidates for Governor, another for U. S. Senator, and so on for all the offices to be filled at that election. This office-group form, known as the Massachusetts ballot, highlights the contest for each office and de-emphasizes party affiliation.

In 27 of the states using the party-column ballot, the voter may place just one mark in an appropriate box at the head of the column of the party he prefers, or pull a single-party lever of a voting machine, and thereby vote for all the candidates nominated by that one political party. Thus, the voter avoids having to make a separate mark for each candidate in the column.

This straight-ticket form of voting, however, is not required. In 20 of these states, the voter who prefers most, but not all, of the candidates of one party may make one mark in the party box or pull the single-party lever and then go on to mark individual votes for the few candidates he supports from the other party. But he need not use the party box or single-party lever at all, if he chooses to "split" his ballot. Only in New Mexico, is the voter required to check a party box before "splitting" his ballot to cast individual votes for candidates of another party. In 6 states, the voter must make a choice: either he votes a straight ticket by casting a single vote for all the candidates of one party, or he passes up this opportunity and votes for individual candidates as he pleases.

Effect of Ballot Forms. These different ballot arrangements can have an impact on election results by enlarging or limiting what is called the "coattail effect." This term refers to the likelihood that voters will support for lesser offices the candidates of the same

---

[2] A few of these states also use a separate ballot for the presidential and vice-presidential candidates.

party whose candidate they support for the highest office at that election. When Eisenhower won in 1952, many voters supported Republican candidates for other offices simply because they had decided to support a Republican for President. Many Democrats won election to Congress in 1964 on the coattails of President Johnson.

The coattail effect will often be strongest in those states that group candidates by party and permit straight-party voting. In these states, the ballot arrangement makes it easy for voters to vote a straight ticket. When the candidate at the head of the ticket wins by a large margin, it is likely that candidates of his party for lesser offices will receive many votes just because they share with him the same party column on the ballot. Of course, local issues and the appeal of local candidates can always have a decisive effect upon contests for local office. A Republican candidate can win a seat in Congress at the same election in which a Democrat over-whelmingly wins the contest for Governor or President in that state. But the local candidate has a more difficult time when the top candidate of the opposition party is very popular and the ballot arrangement permits straight-ticket voting.

A clear example is the outcome of the congressional election contests in Connecticut in 1956 and 1958. In those years the mechanics of the voting machines in that state strongly encouraged straight-ticket voting. Ticket-splitting was possible but difficult: three separate levers had to be moved to split a ticket for just one office.[3] In 1956, Eisenhower scored a huge win in Connecticut, drawing 64% of the vote, even more than his national popular vote margin of 57%. His name at the head of the Republican ticket in Connecticut helped the Republicans to win all 6 congressional seats in that state. Two years later, the highest office on the ballot

---

[3] From 1909 until 1966, voting machines in Connecticut were equipped with a mandatory party lever. The voter was required to use a party lever, which automatically depressed all the individual levers over the names of the candidates of the party selected. To vote for a candidate of another party for one office, the voter first had to "unvote" his party's nominee for that office by raising the individual lever over his name back to its original position, and then depress the individual lever over the name of the other party's candidate.

was the governorship, for a 4-year term. Running for re-election, Abe Ribicoff, the Democratic candidate, won a landslide victory with 62% of the vote. With so many voters pulling the Democratic lever on the voting machines, all 6 congressional candidates of the Democratic Party were elected! This result can be explained only in part by the nationwide Democratic trend in the country that year, which increased the number of Democratic seats in Congress by 21%. But the major cause of the 0 to 6 increase in Democratic Congressmen from Connecticut was the size of Ribicoff's win coupled with the mechanics of the Connecticut voting machines.

Many observers were surprised in 1964 by the election successes of three Republicans: Senator George Murphy, in California; Governor John Volpe, in Massachusetts; and Senator Winston Prouty, who won in Vermont by an unexpectedly large margin. All three were elected in the face of the Johnson landslide. Yet few pointed out that California and Massachusetts require separate votes for each office, and Vermont uses a separate ballot for presidential elections. Thus, in all three states, the format of the ballot substantially lessened the pulling power of President Johnson for other Democratic candidates and gave Republican candidates full opportunity to exploit their own strengths and the opposition's weaknesses to win the support of many Johnson voters.

The fact that all candidates of one party can be voted for by pulling one lever, or marking one box, does not diminish ticket-splitting where a candidate has great personal appeal. In 1964, for example, Republican John Chafee, winning re-election as Governor of Rhode Island, ran an outstanding 42% ahead of the Republican presidential candidate, Barry Goldwater — and the Rhode Island ballot permits straight-party voting. Usually, however, ballot forms seem to make a difference. In 1964, in 21 states which did not permit straight-party voting, 13 Republican candidates for U. S. Senator ran ahead of their presidential nominee by more than 5%. In 12 states which permitted straight-party voting, only 4 Republican Senate candidates ran more than 5% ahead of Goldwater. The ballot form does not cause these results, but it does create opportunities for local candidates to run well against a strong national trend. The ballot that increases the ease of ticket-splitting permits local candidates and issues to have a larger impact on local election results and diminishes the coattail effect of a strong national candidate.

Candidates' Names on the Ballot. Whichever ballot form is used—party-column or office-group—a decision must be made as to the order in which the candidates and parties will be listed. Where party columns are used, often the party whose candidates polled the most votes for statewide office in the last election is entitled to the top row or the first column on the ballot. Many politicians believe this is a favorable location. It is easiest to see, especially on a ballot where several minor parties may be listed. Other techniques include listing the parties alphabetically, choosing the order by lot, and leaving the decision to the official designated to print the ballots.

Where candidates are grouped together by office, the usual practice is to list them alphabetically. Some states list candidates according to their party's statewide vote in the last election. Some list the incumbents first. Still others require that the order of names be rotated throughout the state; for example, if there are four candidates for an office, the name of each would appear as the first name on one-fourth of the ballots in the state.

Election Officials at the Polls. At the polling place, two groups of people have important tasks—the election officials and the party workers. The election officials are responsible for the conduct of the election. Their duties include watching the voting machines or polling booths to guard against any irregularities, ruling on disputes as to whether a person is entitled to vote, checking off the names of those who have voted, and, at the end of the long day, helping to count the votes when the polls have closed. The positions are generally divided between members of the two major parties.

One or more election officials attend every polling place. In some parts of the country, the parties have difficulty recruiting people who are willing to give up a day for such tedious duty. In other areas, the party faithful seek these assignments and the nominal pay that goes with them, and the local precinct leader has a major item of patronage to dispense.

Party Workers at the Polls. Both parties also try to station at least one party worker at each polling place. These workers check, on their own voter lists, the names of those who have voted so that party headquarters can be kept informed, during the day, of the names of those who have not yet voted. In addition, these workers, who often know most of the registered voters in the precinct, stay alert to challenge anyone who might falsely claim to be a person on the list of eligible voters. In some places, these workers are part of the team of election officials.

Campaigning Outside the Polls. Where the party is strong enough in manpower to send more than one worker to each polling place, other workers stand outside the polls, handing out literature to arriving voters. Election laws, generally, require that such last-minute electioneering be kept a minimum distance from the polls, often 75 feet or more. This protective zone scarcely diminishes the effect of on-the-spot campaigning. While voter-decisions are undoubtedly fixed for the major offices by the time people reach the polls, their minds are often wide open on some of the lesser offices for the simple reason that they may not even know who is running. If a familiar face greets them as they approach the polling place, asks them to vote for Jones for city council, and hands them a flyer with an attractive picture of Jones' smiling face and his name prominently written, the chances are good that Jones will get their vote.

One favorite technique used in last-minute campaigning is the sample ballot. Where paper ballots are used, the party workers hand the voters a facsimile of a real ballot, with X's filled in for the candidates the party is supporting. The voter who wishes to follow his party's advice takes the sample ballot with him into the polling booth and uses it as a model for filling out the official ballot. Where voting machines are used, party workers hand out a printed diagram showing how the levers of the machine should be positioned after the voter has voted for the party's choices. The voter then operates the machine, using the diagram as a guide.

Vote Frauds. Every human activity has its share of unlawful conduct, and the business of voting is no exception. Vote frauds are far less frequent today than they were in the past, when flagrant stuffing of a ballot box with fake ballots was not unusual. Even today, unscrupulous people have occasionally voted more than once by using names of deceased voters still on the voting lists. Wholesale frauds have occurred when some election officials have reported false totals of the vote count.

Vote frauds are most likely in those precincts where one party is not represented by any workers or officials, or where the minority party has decided to cooperate in a fraud with the dominant party. Fines and jail sentences await those caught in such frauds. As in so many areas of politics, the best guard against abuses is vigorous competition between the parties in every precinct.

AFTER THE POLLS CLOSE

Counting the Votes.   Just as soon as the polls close, the massive job of counting the votes begins, although a few states permit paper ballots to be counted during the day. Where voting machines are used, the counting task is easy. As each person has voted, each voting machine has automatically kept a running total of votes. At the end of the day, the back of the machine is opened, and the totals for each candidate are ready for reporting. With paper ballots much more work is involved. Election officials must count the ballots and add up the totals themselves. In elections where several offices are being filled, it may be necessary to go through the ballots several times to reach totals for all the candidates for each of the offices. Each precinct reports the vote totals to some central authority, either city or town, county, or state, where totals for the entire election are compiled.

Inevitably mistakes do occur. It is not surprising to find errors of several hundred or more votes, especially where paper ballots are used. If the election outcome is not close, slight errors cause little concern. But where the apparent winner has a bare lead of 100 votes or less in a local contest, or of a few thousand in a statewide contest, the loser often asks for a recount. State laws vary, but, in general, the paper ballots are impounded—held in legal custody so that the recount can be carefully conducted. Voting machines are ordered sealed so that the totals cannot be changed until the recount is completed.

Each House of Congress can conduct recounts of elections of its members. In 1960, Indiana officials at first declared a Republican winner of the Fifth Congressional District by 12 votes. Later, corrections indicated that the Democratic candidate had won by 2

Some ballots are so long and involved that it may take several days before the final results of the election are known.

votes. The Republican went to Washington to claim his seat, but the Democrat asked the House of Representatives to investigate the vote count. The House then ordered a recount, brought the ballots to Washington, and refused to let the Republican take his seat. The recount validated some ballots the state had rejected — for example, those where the voter had marked his ballot with a checkmark instead of an X — and invalidated some ballots the state had counted — for example, a few absentee ballots that had been cast for voters long since deceased. The final result was victory for the Democrat, J. Edward Roush, by a margin of 99 votes.

In modern elections, the press has come to play an important role in the counting and analyzing of election returns. Newspapers, wire services, and radio and television networks now cooperate to station a reporter in almost every precinct in the country in national elections. As soon as the totals are known for the major candidates, reports from each precinct are relayed by telephone to central offices, where statewide and national totals are quickly computed. In 1960, when a margin of slightly more than 100,000 votes separated the two presidential candidates, out of more than 60,000,000 votes cast, the national totals were almost entirely complete 12 hours after the polls closed. Contrast this speed in reporting with the 1916 Presidential election, when several days elapsed before national totals were available to indicate that Wilson had defeated Hughes.

Predicting Results from First Returns.   Modern opinion-polling techniques have recently been used to predict apparent election winners, after just a small fraction of the vote has been counted. Before the election, experts select, in each state, several precincts that include voters of nearly all racial, religious, and economic groups. Then the vote of these precincts in past elections is noted, and the figures put into an electronic computer. As soon as the current returns from these "key" precincts are known, they are also fed into the computer. From a comparison with the vote totals for past elections, the computer instantly calculates what the statewide results will likely be.

For example, consider a state where the Republican candidate for Governor won 47% of the vote in the last election. In three "key" precincts, in that election, he received 30%, 50%, and 70% of the vote. Election-day returns from these same three precincts show the Republican candidate, this year, winning 35%, 55%, and 75% of the vote. This is an increase of 5 percentage points over last time. If the three precincts have been carefully selected, the Republican candidate's percent of the vote will, very likely, increase by the same margin of 5 points throughout the state. Therefore, the analysts will predict victory for the Republican candidate by 52% of the vote.

Such a prediction is made even though the votes from only three precincts have been counted. Using this technique, analysts for the television networks, in 1964, were able to predict with great accuracy the results of the presidential, gubernatorial, and senatorial races in most states, within an hour after the polls closed. Surprisingly these predictions were made when only 2% or 3% of a state's votes had been counted.

"YOU SHOULD SEE THE
EXPRESSIONS ON THEIR FACES"

Bruce Shanks, *Buffalo Evening News*

HI MA!
I WON

James J. Dobbins, *The Boston Herald Traveler*

Analyzing the Votes.   Once the total vote has been counted, a careful analysis will show more than simply who won and who lost. Both the winners and the losers want to know where they made a strong showing and where they ran poorly. A look at the vote in each county, town, ward, and precinct will show detailed results not readily apparent from the total statewide figures. One candidate may have won the election with 51% of the total vote, yet received 80% of the vote in some precincts and only 20% in others. It is important to him to learn as much as he can about the people who live in these precincts so he can tell who his best supporters are and whom he needs more support from next time. For example, the total vote in Georgia was closely divided in the 1964 presidential election, yet examination of precincts in Atlanta with a high Negro population showed that President Johnson won an unprecedented 95% or more of the Negro vote.

To assess a candidate's real strength at the polls you must compare his showing with other candidates of his party in the current election and in previous elections. The fact that a candidate won may prove little about his appeal to the voters if, in fact, candidates of his party always win in this district, and the results show that his margin of victory was less than that of candidates of his party in the past.

Making these comparisons requires some measurement of a candidate's showing at the polls, apart from the basic test of winning or losing. There are three useful figures: a candidate's total vote, his margin of victory or plurality, and his percent of the vote. Whether they win or lose, candidates invariably cite whichever statistic seems to make their showing look best. For example, a losing candidate who polled a very high number of votes will remind party leaders of this fact when he asserts his claim to a nomination next time. He will conveniently ignore the fact that his total vote was due more to population increases and the popularity of the presidential candidate who ran the same year than to his own appeal. Another candidate will claim a big victory by pointing out that he won a statewide election by 100,000 votes. This looks good until you notice that other candidates of his party won their contests in the same state by 200,000 votes.

How well did the candidate really do? His percent of the vote is always the most reliable guide. This statistic provides a sound comparison with other candidates in the same area, with candidates who ran in prior years, and with candidates who ran the same year in other areas. Differences in voter-turnout from one election to another and in number of eligible voters from one state to another lose almost all significance when vote percentages are compared. For example, the candidate who won 55% of the vote in his state for U. S. Senator really did better than the candidate for Governor who won 54% of the vote; or the Senate candidate in the previous election who won 53% of the vote; or the Senate candidate in a neighboring state who won 52% of the vote. Yet, the candidate who polled 55% of the vote might have had less total votes than any of the other three and his margin of victory might have been a smaller number of votes.

The Effect on the Candidates.   Election returns fall with the heaviest impact upon the candidates themselves. The all-or-nothing aspect of a political campaign is overwhelmingly brought home in those brief hours between the closing of the polls and the announcement of the winner. The triumph or tragedy is magnified by the commotion that swirls around the candidate as he awaits the voting

When all the votes are in and victory is assured, the successful candidate (in this photo, Senator Edward Brooke from Massachusetts) comes down to share this moment of glory with his family and all of the people who actively supported him in the campaign.

results. Whether at party headquarters, a hotel suite, or his home, he is usually surrounded by crowds of loyal supporters and workers more ready to share the joy of his victory than to ease the pain of his defeat.

Often the candidate knows the likely outcome and is prepared for the verdict. But if the contest is close, he just has to sit and wait and hope. In a close race both candidates expect to win. Cheering crowds and optimistic friends have convinced them that victory will be theirs.

Finally, at 10 or 11 p.m., or, with a real cliff-hanger, early the next morning, the result is clear. The loser sends a note of congratulations and concession to the winner, thanks his supporters, and is left alone. The winner issues a brief victory statement, thanks his supporters and, much later, is left alone.

These are poignant moments for a political candidate. The loser is deeply disappointed. The work and strain of months have gone for naught. Yet he draws some satisfaction from the type of race he ran, from the amount of support he received, and from the contribution he made to his party. And through the gloom of defeat already breaks the first faint sunlight of victory next time.

For the winner the moment is to be savored. All the effort has been worth it. The weariness of campaigning is dispelled by the exhiliration of triumph. The future, he knows, holds boundless opportunity.

For both winner and loser there is a satisfaction to be shared. Each participated fully in the democratic process. Each in his individual way added something to a system of free government that is one of man's noblest creations. Each left the system stronger than he found it, and by his efforts helped make sure it will endure.

A
FINAL
THOUGHT

January 20, 1961, was an extraordinary day in American politics. That was the day John F. Kennedy was inaugurated as the 35th President of the United States of America. What made the day so special was that few people in the country thought anything exceptional had happened. Of course, everyone knew that a new President was beginning his term of office. There were speeches, parades, and formal balls. But such ceremonies take place in many nations of the world, whenever a new leader takes office.

As a result of an election in which 68,000,000 people voted, control of the most powerful office on earth passed from one political party to the other by a margin of 112,000 votes – just 1/6 of 1% of the total vote! Yet, when Inauguration Day arrived, the leader of the victorious party simply walked into the White House, and the leader of the losing party walked out. In the power centers of government throughout the city of Washington, key officials of the losing party quietly cleaned out their desks and left; key officials of the new administration moved in just as quietly and filled up those desks (on some of which are telephones that can carry orders to unleash the most destructive power the world has ever known). And while this enormous power was being transferred from one political party to another as a result of an eyelash margin of victory at the polls, no one rioted in the streets, no one in the losing party even thought of forcibly retaining office.

In no other country so large and diversified as the United States, and in not many other countries of any size, could transfer of such power have occurred with such complete acceptance by the people. In this country it not only happened, but the acceptance was so complete that few thought anything noteworthy had happened!

This unquestioned transfer of awesome power by virtue of a narrow election victory eloquently states the success of American politics. It is not an achievement to rest on. There are imperfections in our political system. Improvements can and will be made. But we have learned to let the people govern themselves, and we have learned to accept the results. That is the meaning of a day like January 20, 1961 — a meaning of strength, hope, and great promise for the future of American politics.

SUGGESTED READING

Adrian, Charles R. and Charles Press, *The American Political Process.* McGraw-Hill, 1964.

Binkley, Wilfred E., *American Political Parties: Their Natural History.* Alfred A. Knopf, 1959.

Bone, Hugh A., *American Politics and the Party System.* McGraw-Hill, 1965.

Campbell, Angus, Philip E. Converse, Warren E. Miller, and Donald E. Stokes, *The American Voter.* John C. Wiley, 1960.

Chamber of Commerce of the United States, *Action Course in Practical Politics.*

*Clapp, Charles L., *The Congressman: His Work as He Sees It.* The Brookings Institution, 1963.

*Crotty, William J., Donald M. Freeman, and Douglas S. Gatlin, eds., *Political Parties and Political Behavior.* Allyn and Bacon, 1966.

*Dahl, Robert A., *Who Governs? Democracy and Power in an American City.* Yale University Press, 1961.

Hinderaker, Ivan, *Party Politics.* Holt, Rinehart and Winston, 1956.

Key, V. O., Jr., *Politics, Parties, and Pressure Groups.* Thomas Y. Crowell, 1964.

*Lincoln Filene Center for Citizenship and Public Affairs, *Practical Political Action: A Guide for Young Citizens.* Houghton Mifflin, 1962.

Loeb, Marshall and William Safire, *Plunging Into Politics.* David McKay, 1964.

Merriam, Robert E. and Rachel M. Goetz, *Going Into Politics: A Guide for Citizens.* Harper and Row, 1957.

Michener, James A., *Report of a County Chairman.* Random House, 1961.

Nomination and Election of the President and Vice President of the United States including the Manner of Selecting Delegates to National Political Conventions. Document printed for use of the Office of the Secretary of the Senate. United States Government Printing Office, 1964.

Pomper, Gerald, *Nominating the President.* Northwestern University Press, 1963.

Report of the President's Commission on Registration and Voting Participation. United States Government Printing Office, 1963.

Roseboom, Eugene H., *A History of Presidential Elections.* Macmillan, 1964.

*Rossiter, Clinton, *Parties and Politics in America.* Cornell University Press, 1964.

Sait, Edward, *American Parties and Elections,* rev. by Howard R. Penniman. Appleton-Century-Crofts.

*Schattschneider, E. E., *Political Parties and Democracy.* Holt, Rinehart and Winston, 1964.

Shaddeg, Stephen C., *How To Win an Election.* Taplinger, 1964.

*Sorauf, Frank J., *Political Parties in the American System.* Little, Brown, 1964.

Van Riper, Paul P., *Handbook of Practical Politics.* Harper and Row, 1960.

*White, Theodore H., *The Making of the President — 1960.* Atheneum, 1961.

*_____, *The Making of the President — 1964.* Atheneum, 1965.

---

*Available in paperback edition.

INDEX